IT'S ELEMENTARY!

Elementary Grades Task Force Report

Publishing Information

It's Elementary! was developed by the Elementary Grades Task Force and the California Department of Education. (See pages ix–x for the membership of the task force and the names of the principal writer and others who made significant contributions to the document.) The development of *It's Elementary!* was funded by a grant authorized under Chapter 2 of the Elementary and Secondary Education Act. The document was prepared for photo–offset production by the staff of the Bureau of Publications, California Department of Education, working in cooperation with the Department's Elementary Education Office. It was edited for publication by Theodore R. Smith and Sally Wetterholm Smith, and the cover design and interior layout were created by Cheryl Shawver McDonald.

The document was published by the California Department of Education, 721 Capitol Mall, Sacramento, CA 94244-2720. It was printed by the Office of State Printing and distributed under the provisions of the Library Distribution Act and *Government Code* Section 11096.

ISBN 0-8011-1024-6

Copies of *It's Elementary!* are available for $5 each, plus sales tax for California residents, from the Bureau of Publications, Sales Unit, California Department of Education, P.O. Box 271, Sacramento, CA 95812-0271. A partial list of other publications that are available from the Department may be found at the end of this publication. A complete list may be obtained by writing to the address above or by calling the Sales Unit at (916) 445-1260.

CONTENTS

PREFACE

IT'S ELEMENTARY! IS THE REPORT OF THE ELEMENTARY GRADES TASK FORCE convened by the State Superintendent of Public Instruction. This report will reach our schools at a time when there is tremendous ferment in elementary schools throughout the state and nation. *It's Elementary!* is intended to assist teachers, administrators, parents, and community leaders in achieving excellence in public schools during the most critical years of a child's educational development.

Two previous documents—*Here They Come: Ready or Not! The Report of the School Readiness Task Force,* published in 1988, and *Caught in the Middle: Educational Reform for Young Adolescents in California Public Schools,* published in 1987—helped galvanize reform of early childhood and middle grades education, respectively. *It's Elementary!* takes its place between those two documents and will, we hope, have a similar impact—pointing the way for elementary reform efforts in the coming decade.

This report is primarily designed to be used as a road map for the school team of teachers, parents, and administrators. *It's Elementary!* is divided into seven chapters, with each chapter containing recommendations supported by a discussion, excerpts from key writings, and a listing of sources of additional information. The recommendations summarize a great deal of research and practice at the elementary level. Cumulatively, they should help teachers and others engage students from kindergarten through grade six in a thinking curriculum, one which immerses students in a rich learning environment that recognizes and celebrates the unique back- grounds and experiences each student brings to the classroom.

It is important for the reader to understand that in implementing this report, the whole is certainly greater than the sum of its parts. If this were a document whose focus was history, it would speak liberally of "renais- sance" or "enlightenment," the coming together of many ideas at a single point in time. If this were a science document, it might speak of the phe- nomenon of "punctuated equilibrium" where things are stable for a long period of time and then are interrupted by sudden bursts of evolutionary development. In a similar way, elementary education is entering an explo- sive time in terms of new ideas and practice. The recommendations found here will have limited impact if implemented singly. The total improvement of an elementary school program will be much greater, however, when the school community endorses and adopts them in concert. It is simply not enough to approach change eclectically. Rather, students must receive the full benefit of all that teachers know and all that researchers have learned about how to improve the elementary school experience.

The role of teachers is paramount in implementing the recommendations included in this report, for they are the ones who orchestrate learning in the classroom and connect each student to the curriculum. None of the important changes envisioned here will occur unless teachers—supported by site and district administration—have the courage to undertake them. The challenge before us is a great one, but the time is right, for the eyes of the educational community and society at large are focused on elementary education.

SALLY MENTOR
Deputy Superintendent
Curriculum and Instructional
Leadership Branch

FRED TEMPES
Director
Curriculum, Instruction,
and Assessment Division

BARBARA L. BASEGGIO
Administrator
Elementary Education Office

ACKNOWLEDGMENTS

THIS DOCUMENT WAS PREPARED WITH THE HELP OF A TASK FORCE COMPOSED of teachers, administrators, parents, representatives of school boards and parent groups, and others in the educational community. State Superintendent of Public Instruction Bill Honig and members of his staff are most grateful for the efforts and contributions of all of the task force members.

Elementary Grades Task Force

Yvette del Prado, Chairperson, Elementary Grades Task Force; Vice-President of Education and Public Affairs, Tandem Computers

Patricia Almada, Principal, Foster Road Elementary School, Norwalk-La Mirada Unified School District

Gail Anderson, Superintendent, Piedmont Unified School District

Ginger Britt, Project Link Director, Academic Technology Project, Laguna Road School, Fullerton Elementary School District

Jim Brown, Superintendent, Palo Alto Unified School District

Patricia Crocker, Superintendent, Martinez Unified School District

Barbara Daniels, Assistant to the Superintendent, Planning, Development, and Evaluation, Oakland Unified School District

Kevin Davis, Mentor Teacher, Forty-ninth Street School, Los Angeles Unified School District

Linda Davis, Deputy Superintendent, San Francisco Unified School District

Carla B. de Herrera, Bilingual Mentor Teacher, Furgeson Elementary School, ABC Unified School District

Sandra DeYoung, Principal, Lake View Elementary School, Ocean View Elementary School District

Pat Dingsdale, First Vice-President, California State PTA

Antoinette Dunbar, California State Director, Quality Education Project

Madeline Ehrlich, Member, Board of Education, Culver City Unified School District

Linda Espinosa, Director, Primary Education and Child Development Services, Redwood City Elementary School District

Judith S. Gordon, Teacher, Canfield Avenue School, Los Angeles Unified School District

Kenji Hakuta, School of Education, Stanford University

Joyce Hanson, President, Board of Education, Tustin Unified School District

Barbara Hester, Principal, Hickory Elementary School, Torrance Unified School District

Carol Katzman, Assistant Superintendent, Educational Services K-12, Beverly Hills Unified School District

Bill Levinson, Superintendent, Sonoma Valley Unified School District

Luis Martinez, Teacher, Montebello High School, Montebello Unified School District

Lorna Mae Nagata, Assistant Principal, Ramona Elementary School, Alhambra School District

Karen Nemetz, Principal, Mission Avenue Elementary School, San Juan Unified School District

Zoneth Overbey, Principal, Kimbark Elementary School, San Bernardino City Unified School District

Olivia Palacio, Area Superintendent, Fresno High Pyramid, Fresno Unified School District

Mary Jane T. Pearson, Chair, California Commission on Teacher Credentialing

Louise Perez, Member, Board of Education, Sacramento City Unified School District

Marilyn Peterson, Teacher, Laguna Vista Elementary School, Ocean View Elementary School District

Winnie Porter, Bilingual Teacher, Hawthorne Elementary School, San Francisco Unified School District

Cynthia Rathwick, Coordinator, GATE Program, Fresno Unified School District

John Rodriguez, Education Consultant, San Diego

Sharon Rogers, Teacher, Morning Creek Elementary School, Poway Unified School District

Eric Schaps, President, Developmental Studies Center, San Ramon

Susan Van Zant, Principal, Morning Creek Elementary School, Poway Unified School District

Willie Washington, Principal (Ret.), McKinley Avenue School, Los Angeles Unified School District

Gail Yanai, Coordinator, South Shores Visual and Performing Arts Magnet School, Los Angeles Unified School District

Burton Yin, Principal, Lincoln Elementary School, Oakland Unified School District

Principal Writer

William Boly

Research Associates

Claude Goldenberg, Assistant Research Psychologist, Department of Psychiatry, University of California, Los Angeles

Suzanne Sanders, Curriculum Coordinator, Instructional Services, Cupertino Union School District

Barbara Sandman, Education Consultant, Sacramento

Technical Assistance

James Greco, California Department of Education

Adele Solander, California Department of Education

Special Thanks

James R. Smith, Senior Vice President, National Board for Professional Teaching Standards, Detroit, Michigan

John Bernard, Director, Instructional Services, Mount Diablo Unified School District

Betty Hennessy, Consultant, Physical Education, Los Angeles County Office of Education

Donald Kairott, California Department of Education

Patricia Lamson, Superintendent, Cupertino Union School District

Jeffrey Zettel, California Department of Education

INTRODUCTION

"THE START OF ELEMENTARY SCHOOL," AS DEVELOPMENTAL PSYCHOLOGIST Arlene Skolnick has observed, "is in many ways the beginning of the child's adult career." Because what happens during the early years lays a foundation for all that follows, the elementary grades may well be the most influential in any individual's formal educational experience.

The years from kindergarten through grade six are a time of uninhibited wonder, enthusiasm for learning, and breathtakingly rapid growth. The social, emotional, physical, and intellectual identities children construct for themselves during this period go a long way toward determining the subsequent trajectories of their lives. Are California's elementary schools taking full advantage of this unique developmental window of opportunity? Are they helping all children—irrespective of ethnic, cultural, linguistic, or socioeconomic background or disability—get the best possible start in life? What constitutes excellent practice in the elementary school in light of the changing conditions of modern society as well as the latest findings from research? The purpose of *It's Elementary!* is to address these questions; to examine what an outstanding California elementary school of the 1990s might look like; and to make specific recommendations for realizing that vision.

> The purpose of *It's Elementary!* is to examine what an outstanding California elementary school of the l990s might look like.

Why Change Elementary Education?

This is a particularly good time to take a close look at elementary education in California for three principal reasons. And each of these reasons has to do with fundamental change—in the make-up of the student population; in society's expectations about what elementary school should accomplish; and in our understanding of how children learn.

The Changing School Population

Today's children bring a rich mix of experiential, ethnic, linguistic, religious, and cultural backgrounds to the schoolhouse door—differences whose nuances must be recognized, appreciated, and accommodated by the instructional program. Over half of California's elementary school-age children are Hispanic, black, or Asian. One out of six students was born in another country. Children from over 80 different language groups who are learning English as a new language[1] make up a full 29 percent of students entering kindergarten in California.[2]

In socioeconomic terms, today's children come from a variety of family structures far different from the stereotypical father-as-breadwinner, mother-as-homemaker pattern of yesteryear. In the majority of two-parent families, both parents work outside the home. Divorce in all segments of society has become more common than it once was: as many as 60 percent of California's children may be part of a home headed by a single parent at some time before reaching age eighteen.[3]

Many children are coming to school healthier and wealthier than ever before. These children may have spent two years or longer in developmentally appropriate preschool programs and, thus, enjoy an early learning base that the elementary school can build on and extend. Because of insufficient public funding, however, many children from low-income households do not have this opportunity. Indeed, a growing economic disparity, largely along racial–ethnic lines, is becoming increasingly evident in California. The number of children in the state living in poverty doubled between 1969 and 1987, and if current trends persist, one out of every three children will be living in poverty by the year 2000.[4] The incidence of child abuse, neglect, hunger, and homelessness has also increased markedly in the past

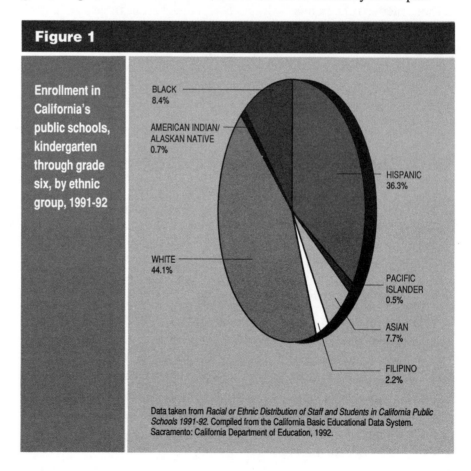

Figure 1

Enrollment in California's public schools, kindergarten through grade six, by ethnic group, 1991-92

BLACK
8.4%

AMERICAN INDIAN/
ALASKAN NATIVE
0.7%

HISPANIC
36.3%

WHITE
44.1%

PACIFIC
ISLANDER
0.5%

ASIAN
7.7%

FILIPINO
2.2%

Data taken from *Racial or Ethnic Distribution of Staff and Students in California Public Schools 1991-92.* Compiled from the California Basic Educational Data System. Sacramento: California Department of Education, 1992.

decade. Stanford University Law Professor Michael Wold estimates that 15 percent of babies born in the public hospitals of California's major cities are addicted to drugs or alcohol.[5] These children are now arriving in elementary school classrooms in substantial numbers.

Changing Expectations for the Elementary School

The mission of California's elementary schools is to nurture the intellectual, physical, emotional, and moral capacities of each child to the fullest extent possible so that each can profit by continued schooling and so that, ultimately, each can lead a fulfilling life in our society as a productive worker, citizen, and private individual. What does this mean in contemporary terms? The service and technology-driven global economy of the twenty-first century will demand a much higher level of intellectual attainment for a far greater percentage of workers than did the smokestack and agriculture-dominated one of the past. American business leaders have been telling educators that they seek employees who not only can read and compute but also can think creatively and critically and adapt to change.

An urgency similar to the need to help students prepare for tomorrow's workplace faces our schools in educating good citizens and responsible adults. As California becomes more cosmopolitan and diverse, fostering an understanding and allegiance to the principles that bind its citizens together as a society becomes absolutely crucial. Part of this growth will come from academic learning; but an even greater part will come from the day-to-day example of the school as a caring community. In well-run classrooms, students absorb invaluable lessons about developing tolerance for others and mutual respect, about cooperating to achieve a team's goals, and about gaining a love for learning that will last a lifetime. The internalization of such essential values as honesty, fairness, generosity, compassion, and a humane reverence for life constitutes a vital, if too often unstated, part of the school curriculum.

"... the entire educational program must be reconceived and revitalized so that thinking pervades students' lives from kindergarten onward..."

Lauren Resnik and Leopold Klopfer

The Changing View of How Children Learn

Recent advances in cognitive psychology—the science of how we learn—also have profound implications for the elementary school curriculum. The traditional grade school curriculum consisted of a hierarchical sequence of basic academic skills that students were expected to acquire, often through dogged practice. This approach reflected a view of children as empty vessels that the teacher filled up with knowledge by pouring in an agreed-on inventory of skills in an agreed-on order (from simple to complex, with the most complex "skills" of thinking and problem solving reserved for the later years of education). But modern cognitive research has found that children are actually more like natural scientists bent on making sense of the world. According to this view, all children are quite capable of sophisticated thought processes from the beginning of their formal education. Indeed, they truly learn *only* when they are afforded the opportunity to actively incorporate what they are studying into their own experiences, concepts, and understandings of how the world works. This insight has many practical implications in the classroom, the most important of which is, as Lauren Resnick and Leopold Klopfer wrote in *Toward the Thinking Curriculum*:

> . . . the entire educational program must be reconceived and revitalized so that thinking pervades students' lives from kindergarten onward, in mathematics and history class, in reading and science, in composition and art, in vocational and special education.[6]

Who Is This Report For?

Taken together, the trends described above point to an obvious conclusion: in an era of scarce financial resources, California's elementary schools are being asked to fundamentally reinvent themselves. The process of managing this deep, systemic change reaches in to every aspect of the educational enterprise and seeks the active involvement of every person with an interest in public education: teachers, students, support staff, administrators, parents, community members, and business leaders. Change cannot be imposed from the top. Professionals at the school site must be given the opportunity and time to digest the various ideas found here, experiment with them in their own classrooms, discuss the results with their peers, reject those that do not work, and adapt those that do to their own teaching styles. On the other hand, large-scale change will not take place without the blessing and support of a school district's leaders, parents, and other concerned parties.

To reach the ambitious goal of providing a rich and rigorous education to all students, a long-term effort will be required that redefines every aspect of elementary education—curriculum, pedagogy, assessment, governance, professional roles, and allocation of resources. *It's Elementary!* certainly is not intended as the last word on all these subjects. Rather, the Elementary Grades Task Force has conceived of this document as a syllabus that teachers and all those concerned with public education can work through to evaluate their own practices and plot a course for classroom, school, and system-wide improvement. While discussions of the various recommendations put forward here have been kept necessarily brief, topics in the report are followed by a set of selected references for those seeking more detailed information.

What Is the Content of the Report?

It's Elementary! is divided into seven chapters. Each chapter consists of an introductory statement followed by a series of recommendations and discussions. Vignettes, graphics, and excerpts from seminal writings highlight important points.

- Chapter 1, "The Thinking Curriculum in the Elementary Years," includes a discussion of current learning theory in detail and a discussion of the changes it implies for elementary instruction on a subject-by-subject basis.
- Chapter 2, "In the Classroom," deals with practical strategies for implementing a rigorous curriculum. It considers the two main misgivings teachers have about making the transition to the thinking curriculum: how to find the time to do it all and how to manage the diversity of learning backgrounds among students while in the process.
- Chapter 3, "All in the Profession," concerns ways to connect classroom teachers to the larger professional issues in kindergarten through grade six. It highlights the importance of budgeting significant time in the school year for staff development on curricular issues.
- Chapter 4, "Measures for Success," includes a description of how the elementary grades assessment program can be turned into a powerful spur to curricular reform.
- Chapter 5, "Creation of a Learning Environment," outlines ways to build the emotional bond among family, child, and school, thereby creating the "caring communities" that are so characteristic of successful schools.
- Chapter 6, "Coordinating Student Services," addresses the overlay of physical and emotional needs that an increasing number of students bring with them to schools and maps out a strategy to help these children, with the school acting as a clearinghouse and health care professionals combining efforts in a coordinated multiagency response.
- Chapter 7, "Organizing to Meet the Challenge," includes a description of steps school districts and their governing boards can take to support elementary schools in their quest to improve themselves.

Can We Make a Difference?

Throughout their deliberations, it became clear that the Elementary Grades Task Force members shared two beliefs about elementary education. The first was that all students can learn. The second was that good schools make a tremendous difference in ensuring that students do learn. Every year recipients of the competitive California Distinguished Schools Award include a number of excellent schools with majority–minority student populations located in low-income neighborhoods. How did these schools overcome the defeatist expectations? What is the secret of their success? No quality has been more critical than the fact that teachers and parents at these schools have refused to take failure for an answer. Merely providing access to improved curriculum and instruction is not enough. Students at these schools are expected to work hard and achieve; more often than not, they rise to the challenge.

Good schools, as the Task Force learned repeatedly, make a huge difference in the lives of the children who attend them. The Task Force and the California Department of Education hope that the ideas presented here hasten the day when all California's children have access to such schools and to a great start in their elementary years.

For Further Information

"Explosive Growth, Dramatic Change for California Kids—and a Worsening Future Without Drastic Intervention," *Stanford Educator* (spring/summer, 1989), 1.

Kirst, Michael W., and others. *Conditions of Children in California.* Berkeley: Policy Analysis for California Education (PACE), 1989.

Olsen, Laurie. *Crossing the Schoolhouse Border: Immigrant Students and the California Public Schools.* San Francisco and Los Angeles: California Tomorrow Project, 1988.

Resnick, Lauren. *Education and Learning to Think.* Washington, D.C.: National Academy Press, 1987.

Toward the Thinking Curriculum: Current Cognitive Research. 1989 Yearbook of the Association for Supervision and Curriculum Development. Edited by Lauren Resnick and Leopold Klopfer. Alexandria, Va.: Association for Supervision and Curriculum Development, 1989.

THE THINKING CURRICULUM IN THE ELEMENTARY YEARS

THE CALIFORNIA EDUCATIONAL REFORM MOVEMENT BEGAN WITH A FOCUS on middle and high school reform. But the growing weight of evidence suggests that key changes in elementary education are also needed.

In California, elementary students over the last ten years have significantly improved their scores in all areas of the California Assessment Program, even though steady gains recorded through the mid-1980s have tended to plateau or taper off slightly since 1987-88. Third and sixth graders in the state have often scored higher than their national counterparts on measures of their reading, writing, and mathematics prowess. These encouraging signs should not lull anyone into a false sense of complacency, however. For one thing, thirteen-year-olds in the U.S., who are the end product of our elementary schools, consistently finish near the bottom in international comparisons of their understanding of mathematics and science. (See Figure 2.) More to the point, though, many standardized tests do not tell whether schools are providing the education our students need to succeed in the twenty-first century. Rather, such tests tend to assess what most elementary schools have concentrated on in the past: teaching basic skills in the three Rs.

The Nature of the Problem

Numerous studies of typical classroom practice suggest that elementary education in the United States could be improved significantly.[1] In particular, the most pervasive problem afflicting much elementary instruction in the past has been a narrow focus on the acquisition of discrete academic skills—the ability to decode a word, punctuate a sentence, do long division, identify the parts of a flower—to the exclusion of more thought-provoking content exploration that taps the child's real-world experiences, feelings, and interests. Too often, children are fed a steady diet of teacher recitation, drill, and rote exercises instead of opportunities to solve problems and creatively express ideas and concepts. And the problem is not limited to elementary schools. In its 1988 report, *Here They Come, Ready or Not*, the California School Readiness Task Force identified the pushing down of such skill-focused academic programs into the kindergarten and preschool years and the inappropriate reliance on passive rote learning as major concerns in need of corrective action.

The original rationale for the basic skills curriculum was rooted in earlier educational theory which held that students had to learn to crawl intellectually before they could walk or run. But the application of the theory has been disappointing. Singleminded concentration on the mechanics of reading and mathematics, to the exclusion of how these subjects can inform and stimulate children's everyday understanding of the world, has discouraged students' interest in school. Confronted with a dull, repetitious,

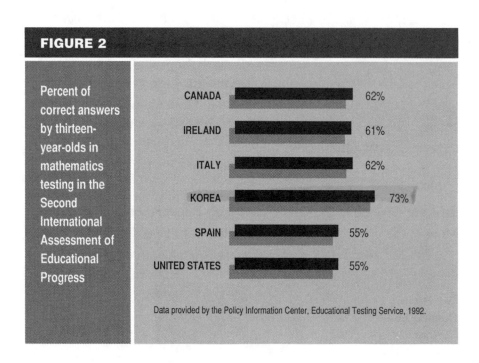

FIGURE 2

Percent of correct answers by thirteen-year-olds in mathematics testing in the Second International Assessment of Educational Progress

CANADA 62%
IRELAND 61%
ITALY 62%
KOREA 73%
SPAIN 55%
UNITED STATES 55%

Data provided by the Policy Information Center, Educational Testing Service, 1992.

and uninspiring curriculum, many children react by withdrawing into a kind of intellectual passive resistance. As recent studies have repeatedly shown, underachieving children begin to drop out mentally around the fourth grade, many years before they drop out physically.

The Solution: The Thinking Curriculum

Children are seekers of meaning. No sooner do they learn how to talk than they begin asking questions about simple things as well as about the dilemmas of human existence that have perplexed philosophers and theologians from the dawn of time. Children are intensely interested in exploring questions of values, feelings, meaning, and the relationship of self to others. A curriculum that addresses these questions engages a child intellectually more than a skills-based one because it takes advantage of the natural curiosity and sense-making drive that motivate the child toward effortful performance.

The thinking curriculum does *not* call for the end of direct instruction or the learning of facts. Nor does it deny the importance of mastering traditional academic skills. What it does say, however, is that these skills are best acquired in the context of meaningful learning experiences that harness the child's inquisitive nature to the task at hand. Learning how to think and learning subject-matter content are not separate processes; rather, they are two facets of the same invaluable intellectual gem.

California's subject-matter frameworks and model curriculum guides were recast in the 1980s to be consistent with current research on how children learn. Organized by subject, the frameworks collectively present a fundamentally new vision of what a model elementary school curriculum should include. Qualitatively, they call for a shift from a skills-based pedagogy in which the teacher serves as the dispenser of knowledge to a hands-on, student-centered, experiential one. Quantitatively, they call for a greater depth of understanding in a wider range of knowledge areas than ever before attempted at the elementary level. The remainder of this chapter includes a brief summary of the critical concepts from each of the main subject areas as they apply at the elementary level.

Children are seekers of meaning. No sooner do they learn how to talk than they begin asking questions about the simplest things as well as about the dilemmas of human existence that have perplexed philosophers and theologians from the dawn of time.

For Further Information

Lewis, Anne C. "Getting Unstuck: Curriculum as a Tool of Reform," *Phi Delta Kappan*, Vol. 71 (March, 1990), 534–538.

Poplin, Mary. "The Quest for Meaning," *The Claremont Reading Conference Yearbook*. Edited by Malcolm P. Douglass. Claremont, Calif.: The Claremont Center for Developmental Studies, 1986.

Resnick, Lauren. *Education and Learning to Think*. Washington, D.C.: National Academy Press, 1987.

Toward the Thinking Curriculum: Current Cognitive Research. 1989 Yearbook of the Association for Supervision and Curriculum Development. Edited by Lauren Resnick and Leopold Klopfer. Alexandria, Va.: Association for Supervision and Curriculum Development, 1989.

Language Arts in the Elementary Years

The language arts curriculum should be organized around compelling literary works. A steady diet of literature from the earliest years can provide the child with significant content through which the language competencies of listening, speaking, reading, and writing can be developed in an integrated and meaning-centered fashion.

In the primary grades, one of the key responsibilities of schools is to teach children how to read and write; in the intermediate grades, it is to help children gain fluency and confidence in reading and writing so that they can learn. Each of these responsibilities poses a special set of challenges.

Initial literacy. In the early grades, the dominant mode of reading instruction in most elementary schools has been phonics. Although phonics is a valuable tool for a beginning reader, this approach sometimes has received so much emphasis that inadequate time has been spent on the essential purpose of reading: making meaning from text. Phonics is an important element in the teaching of reading, but it should never be allowed to become the whole program.

The best approach in the instruction of all novice readers and writers is to create a rich environment, steeped in authentic language and stimulating stories that vitally connect with what the children already know and are

---

A Curriculum for All

The thinking curriculum is not a course to be added to a crowded program when time permits. It is not a program that begins after the basics have been mastered or the facts memorized. It is not a program reserved for a minority of students, such as the gifted or the college bound. The thinking curriculum calls for recognition that all real learning involves thinking, that thinking ability can be nurtured and cultivated in everyone, and that the entire educational program must be reconceived and revitalized so that thinking pervades students' lives beginning in kindergarten.

Quoted with permission from "Assessing the Thinking Curriculum: New Tools for Educational Reform" by Lauren B. Resnick and Daniel P. Resnick in *Changing Assessments: Alternative Views of Aptitude, Achievement and Instruction.* Edited by Bernard R. Gifford and Mary Catherine O'Connor. Boston: Kluwer Academic Publishers, 1992, p. 40.

Seatwork vs. Silent Reading

Most students in the elementary grades spend the majority of time allocated to reading instruction doing "seatwork"—filling in the blanks in workbooks that accompany the basal reading program. It is not uncommon for a child to bring home 1,000 workbook pages and skill sheets completed during a reading period in the course of his or her elementary grades career. But the completion of skill sheets does *not* necessarily promote reading proficiency. Research shows that a far more productive use of classroom time is to have regularly scheduled silent reading opportunities in which children practice the whole skill of reading. The National Commission on Reading has recommended that two hours a week should be available for independent reading by the time children reach the third or fourth grade.[2]

curious about. Literature offers children both the vivid language and compelling plots of the time-tested classics and the good contemporary works that they find inherently fascinating.

In general, successful initial literacy programs:

1. Regularly expose students to the best in children's literature.
2. Provide students ample opportunities for developing oral language by encouraging them to discuss their thoughts and ideas about stories they have heard as well as about the world around them.
3. Introduce students to writing by providing them opportunities to dictate individual and group stories, which are written and then read aloud.
4. Recognize each student's level of preparedness for reading and build on that base.
5. Stimulate children's interpretive thought processes by focusing on comprehension with strategic discussions and questioning before, during, and after readings.
6. Include a phonics component that is presented early and kept simple.
7. Stress the connection between what is written and the child's real world experiences.
8. Strike a healthy balance between oral and silent reading practice.
9. Integrate practice in the other language skills of writing, listening, and speaking.
10. Encourage parents to read aloud to their children, take them to the library, and discuss stories and events with them.

Extending reading fluency. Once children have learned to make meaning from the printed word and understand simple, well-written stories, they can begin to build confidence and fluency in their new reading skill. Typically, reading proficiency has been developed in the elementary years by means of basal reading programs, complete packages of commercially produced instructional materials that include graded anthologies of abridged reading selections, workbooks and skill sheets, and teachers' manuals with accompanying instructional strategies and materials. Researchers estimate that basal reading programs account for from 75 to 90 percent of what takes place during reading periods in most elementary school classrooms.[3]

Such an overreliance on a prepackaged curriculum compromises the quality of the reading program in two ways. First, basal textbooks can be bland and vacuous. Governed as they are by rigid readability formulas, most basal reading selections are simply not as interesting as the literature available for children of the same age. Second, the accompanying exercises rarely ask students to think about what they have read. More often the exercises seem designed to mark time with monotonous "circle the M's and P's" work sheets.

Good elementary reading programs recognize that reading is not a subject in itself so much as it is a tool of discovery that students can use to enter enticing new worlds. Skill in reading is acquired and perfected by practicing it across the curriculum—in mathematics, history–social sciences, and science. In those subject areas, the emphasis in reading is kept where it belongs—on reading for meaning—rather than on the mechanics of the operation.

Regular "read aloud" sessions in which the teacher reads to students are indispensable in keeping the focus on reading for meaning. Because the teacher does the code-breaking, reading aloud gives all students in the class, even those with poor reading skills, the opportunity to enjoy literature. The teacher can directly model comprehension strategies for students as he or she reads, taking them on a "walk through the mind"—wondering about characters' motives, figuring out the meaning of a word from its context, making connections to one's own life, predicting what will happen next. Demonstrating how an expert reader approaches a text is also one of the most effective ways that teachers and parents can help children learn successful comprehension strategies.

Of course, it must be remembered that reading is only one of the language arts skills. Language development in terms of listening, speaking, reading, and writing is an integrated process in which gains in any single area contribute to gains in all the rest. Writing activities, in particular, can powerfully contribute to reading proficiency, especially when teachers have children communicate in a variety of ways to real audiences. Reading is

Good elementary reading programs recognize that reading is not a subject in itself so much as it is a tool of discovery that students can use to enter enticing new worlds.

crucial to the ability to write, and systematic reading and writing instruction in many different modes of discourse is central to children's intellectual development. Unlike skill-sheet seatwork, writing can involve students in original thinking about the material they have just read and, consequently, can stretch their mental processes in beneficial ways. A knowledge of punctuation, spelling, and grammar is important because it facilitates written communication to a broad public; but it is not the first competency a child must master in learning how to write nor should it be treated as an instructional end in itself.

The best elementary language arts programs sustain an atmosphere in which reading is perceived as a joyful experience. Using texts rich with interesting ideas and information, moving through them at an appropriate pace, and arranging for high rates of success can all help attain the ultimate goal: the development of lifelong readers.

For Further Information

Becoming a Nation of Readers. Prepared by Richard C. Anderson and others. Washington, D.C.: The National Institute of Education, 1984.

English–Language Arts Framework for California Public Schools: Kindergarten Through Grade Twelve. Prepared by the English–Language Arts Curriculum Framework and Criteria Committee. Sacramento: California Department of Education, 1987.

English–Language Arts Model Curriculum Guide. Sacramento: California Department of Education, 1988.

Jager-Adams, Marilyn. *Beginning to Read: Thinking and Learning About Print.* Center for the Study of Reading. Urbana, Ill.: The University of Illinois at Urbana–Champaign, 1990.

Recommended Readings in Literature: Kindergarten Through Grade Eight. Prepared by the Language Arts and Foreign Languages Unit. Sacramento: California Department of Education, 1986; annotated version, 1988.

Recommended Readings in Spanish Literature, Kindergarten Through Grade Eight. Sacramento: California Department of Education, 1991.

Report Card on Basals. Urbana, Ill.: National Council of Teachers of English, 1988.

Tharp, Roland, and Ronald Gallimore. "Rousing Schools to Life," *American Educator*, Vol. 13 (Summer, 1989), 20–25, 46–52.

Mathematics in the Elementary Years

Mathematics as commonly presented in today's elementary schools has been described as a "curriculum out of balance."[4] Researchers point to a heavy emphasis on rote mastery of computational skills on the one hand and scant attention to creatively exploring mathematical concepts derived from the child's everyday experiences on the other. In sharp contrast with other

How Old Are You?

Once students learn to rely on procedures, they tend to give up on common sense. For example, students may initially learn multiplication by understanding it as a series of repeated additions, but then lose that original meaning after being taught the routine procedures for two- and three-digit multiplication and applying them repeatedly. Students can quote the steps about "crossing out and moving over" as well as recite rules, but they no longer have an idea whether their answers are reasonable. This can lead to preposterous answers and does little to prevent rote implementation of computational procedures based on misconceptions. For example, one child systematically excluded zero from all her computations because "zero doesn't count for anything" until she was asked to think about her age, which would one day be 10.

Quoted with approval from *The Mathematics Report Card* by John A. Dossey and others. Princeton, N.J.: Educational Testing Service, 1988, p. 67.

In exemplary mathematics programs, students are given opportunities to construct their own mathematical understandings from open-ended encounters with challenging situations.

countries, a large portion of the elementary mathematics curriculum in the United States every year after kindergarten is little more than a rehash of material covered previously.

In exemplary mathematics programs, students are not sentenced to endlessly repeating procedures that produce single, correct answers; rather, they are given opportunities to construct their own mathematical understandings from open-ended encounters with challenging situations. Students experience mathematics as a way of interpreting the world around them, figuring out how to share fairly a plate of cookies, comparing how much different containers hold, finding the "best buy" at the supermarket, deciding how much food to purchase for a birthday party. Students choose hand calculators, manipulatives, or other tools to use while they work. They frequently work together, sharing numerical estimates and discussing their ideas about how to find answers. Students explain their thinking, orally and in writing, and build their understanding of mathematics over a long period of time.

Most students establish their lifelong attitudes towards mathematics in the elementary grades. All too often, initial positive attitudes plummet by the time students reach sixth grade. This trend represents a loss of talent our state can ill afford. Many scientific and business careers require a solid foundation in mathematics. It is particularly important that females, black, and Hispanic students become comfortable at an early age with the full range of thinking in mathematics so that they will not be excluded later from the many opportunities that mathematical power affords. The key to improvement in this area lies in changing the elementary mathematics curriculum—from one that emphasizes correctly following procedures to arrive at the "right" answer to one that presents mathematics as a way to explore and gain control over situations in the real world.

For Further Information

Everybody Counts: A Report to the Nation on the Future of Mathematics Education. Prepared under the direction of the National Research Council. Washington, D.C.: National Academy Press, 1989.

Mathematics Framework for California Public Schools, Kindergarten Through Grade Twelve, 1992. Sacramento: California Department of Education. In press.

Mathematics Model Curriculum Guide. Sacramento: California Department of Education, 1987.

McKnight, Curtis, and others. *The Underachieving Curriculum: Assessing U.S. School Mathematics from an International Perspective.* Report of the International Association for the Evaluation of Educational Achievement. Champaign, Ill.: Stipes Publishing Company, 1987.

Paulo, John Allen. *Innumeracy: Mathematical Illiteracy and Its Consequence.* New York: Hill and Wang, 1988.

Porter, Andrew. "A Curriculum Out of Balance—The Case of Elementary School Mathematics," *Educational Research*, Vol. 18 (June-July, 1989), 9–15.

Steen, Lynn Arthur. "Teaching Mathematics for Tomorrow's World," *Educational Leadership*, Vol. 4 (September, 1989), 18–23.

Thurston, William P. *Mathematical Education: Notices of the American Mathematical Society*, Vol. 37 (September, 1990), 844–850.

Willoughby, Stephen S. *Mathematics Education for a Changing World.* Alexandria, Va.: Association for Curriculum and Supervision Development, 1990.

History–Social Science in the Elementary Years

A strong history–social science program at the elementary level helps all students to develop their full potential for personal, civic, and professional life. The elementary curriculum is centered in a core of historical and geographical knowledge, integrating the social sciences and humanities, with an emphasis on ethics and democratic values. It helps students to better understand themselves and others and to develop judgment, perception, civic pride, and responsibility.

A variety of materials, resources, primary sources, strategies, and technologies are used to engage students. This variety fosters enjoyment of history, cultivating historical empathy for and a knowledge of men, women, and children of different times, places, and cultures. Much of the literature used to enhance history studies in kindergarten through grade six should emphasize heroes, adventure, moral challenges, faraway places, and distant times so that students' imaginations are captivated, broadening the perspec-

Much of the literature used to enhance history studies in kindergarten through grade six should emphasize heroes, adventure, moral challenges, faraway places, and distant times so that students' imaginations are captivated.

tive they have on their nation and the world and inspiring them through examples of ethical behavior.

The curriculum in the primary grades follows what has been called a "here-there-then" approach. Each year of instruction begins in the child's immediate present and then moves outward in space and back in time to enrich his or her geographical and historical understanding. For instance, second graders might begin by studying people in the local community who produce, process, and distribute food. Next, they might learn how trade and transportation link the local community with other food-producing communities in Central America or Africa. Finally, they might study the ways people of long ago ground grain, baked bread, and refrigerated foods. The study is enriched by the use of such books as *Bananas from Manolo to Margie* or *Fannie's Fruits,* integrating geography and economics with history. Specific units of study described in the *History–Social Science Framework* ensure that youngsters receive a sequential program which progresses over the span from kindergarten through grade three.

In the intermediate grades specific content and time periods are identified for study. In grade four students build on learnings from the primary grades in the study of California history, including not only the more traditional topics but also California's recent past and current circumstances. A formal study of United States history and geography is begun in fifth grade, with special emphasis given to people and events up to circa 1850, including not only chronological topics but also major themes of national identity and democratic heritage and ideas.

The world history program at sixth grade emphasizes people and events in ancient civilizations, both Western and non-Western. It is particularly important that fifth and sixth grade teachers understand how the curriculum they teach relates to seventh and eighth grade courses. The sixth and seventh grades' focus on world history, for example, is intended to give entering eighth graders a broader understanding of the global context from which the United States grew. Some coordination with middle schools is therefore necessary to achieve the necessary focus and continuity.

The elementary program contains opportunities for interdisciplinary studies, enriched with primary sources, varied genres of literature—both of the period and about the period—and the visual and performing arts. Throughout the grades, the program engenders those "habits of mind" unique to history–social science. Among these are an understanding of events over time, providing students with examples from human experience; a deeper understanding of change and continuity, including the values and problems inherent in both; a keener examination of human action, beliefs, ideas, issues, and ways of life; a firmer grasp of the democratic heritage on which our multiethnic nation is founded; and a beginning

The elementary program contains opportunities for interdisciplinary studies, enriched with primary sources, varied genres of literature—both of the period and about the period—and the visual and performing arts.

Time and Space

Dates are not meaningful concepts for primary grade children who lack the mathematical concepts to understand them. But young children *can* think historically—particularly when they are helped to develop a spatial sense of time's passage through such visual aids as time lines. Such devices need not be elaborate. One California teacher makes creative use of a clothesline and clothespins. Children first tie a knot near one end of the clothesline to represent "today" and clip on a recent photo of themselves. They move back a few inches to attach a baby picture. After the teacher reads a biography of Martin Luther King, Jr. to the class, the children make drawings illustrating the Reverend King's life and clip them to the line farther back in time. Other famous historical figures are placed at appropriate intervals. Inevitably, the subject of dinosaurs comes up. Children decide these precursors of the human story should occupy a place on the time line long, long, long ago.

Adapted from "History Is for Children" by Charlotte Crabtree. Reprinted with permission from the winter, 1989, issue of *American Educator*, the quarterly journal of the American Federation of Teachers, p. 38.

understanding of the common ideals embodied in rights, responsibilities, and the historic struggle to achieve equality and freedom for all.

For Further Information

Building a History Curriculum: Guidelines for Teaching History in School. Westlake, Ohio: Bradley Commission on History in Schools, 1988.

Course Models for the History–Social Science Framework: United States History and Geography—Making a New Nation (for Grade Five). Sacramento: California Department of Education, 1991.

Crabtree, Charlotte. "History is for Children," *American Educator,* Vol. 13 (Winter, 1989), 34–43.

Historical Literacy. Edited by Paul Gagnon. New York: Macmillan Publishing Co., 1989.

History–Social Science Framework for California Public Schools: Kindergarten Through Grade Twelve. Prepared by the History–Social Science Curriculum Framework and Criteria Committee. Sacramento: California Department of Education, 1987.

Literature for History–Social Science, Kindergarten Through Grade Eight. Compiled by the History–Social Science and Visual and Performing Arts Unit. Sacramento: California Department of Education, 1991.

Ravitch, Diane. "Tot Sociology," *American Scholar*, Vol. 56 (Summer, 1987), 343–54.

With History–Social Science for All: Access for Every Student. Sacramento: California Department of Education, 1992.

Science in the Elementary Years

Science is more than a collection of facts about the natural world; it is a way of thinking, of approaching problems objectively by theorizing about what might be from careful observation of what is, and then testing the hypothesis. Science in the elementary grades should help all students learn how to think as scientists think, even as they become familiar with the laws and principles that govern the natural world.

In the elementary grades, a basic problem facing science instruction is the need to achieve curricular parity with reading, writing, or mathematics. In many classrooms, the science period remains the one most likely to be dropped when lessons in other subjects run past their allotted times. Time constraints comingle with a lack of confidence among many elementary teachers to limit instruction in science. According to a survey by the National Science Teachers Association, 82 percent of elementary teachers feel qualified to teach reading, but only 27 percent feel qualified to teach either

Forty Birds: A Lesson from the Boy Scouts

If we are serious about our current discussions of school change, we need to think about curricula that promote good teaching and real learning instead of continuing with practices that encourage our students to associate mastery of a subject with the recognition of little bits of information. As I look around for curriculum models that illustrate such a shift in perspective, an experience I had as a youngster in the Boy Scouts comes to mind.

Boy Scouts of America, after all, is an educational institution. It has a curriculum, and it promotes kids who follow the curriculum from Tenderfoot to Second Class, and on up to Eagle Scout. But its curriculum and testing practices are very different from those found in schools. Take my experience with the bird-study merit badge, the experience of a city kid who wasn't very interested in birds.

If I had learned about birds in school, my teacher probably would have had flashcards and pictures of birds all over the room. She would have assigned us chapters in a textbook to read, and eventually, she would have given us a test for which we would have had to match up bird names with bird pictures and fill in the blanks in some kind of chart. I know I would have forgotten the birds within three weeks of taking the test—and that would have been no loss because I would probably have learned to hate birds.

But in the Boy Scouts, you actually have to see forty different kinds of birds, *see* them. And you don't do it by looking out your window or taking a walk through the park. You've got to get up at five o'clock in the morning physical or earth/space science.[5] Assigning instruction in science a secondary role also reflects a conviction that elementary students are too young to understand scientific reasoning. But nothing could be further from the truth. From the time they can walk and talk, children ask questions about cause and effect; about what makes things happen. In that respect they are the original natural scientists, constantly engaged in sense-making activity.

In the elementary grades, young students should be *doing* science in their classrooms, not merely reading about it. California's *Science Framework* recommends that 40 percent of the total time spent learning science should be in activity-based lessons. At the same time, however, the best "hands-on" activities must also be "minds-on." Simply having students do science—by having them follow an experiment in cookbook fashion—will not lead them to new understandings if their interests and intellects are not also engaged. For example, researchers assessed students' conceptual understandings of photosynthesis after an eight-week unit of 24 lessons in

so you can be in a swamp as the sun is about to come up. Or you have to go at sunset to a hill or a mountain. And, of course, since you probably don't want to go all by yourself, you invite a couple of your best friends.

When you look through your binoculars at a bird in flight, it doesn't look like a stuffed bird in a museum. What is it? To find out, you look through the field guide with your buddies. You say, "There it is; that's the one." And one of your friends says, "No! That says Texas; we're in New York." So you keep looking until you find a bird that fits all the things you saw. And you do that for 40 birds.

The final test is simple: You take a walk with one or two people who really know birds, and you spot every bird. That's the kind of knowledge that doesn't leave you because you've actively participated in gaining it. It's become part of you. I don't know anyone who got a *bird-study merit badge* who *hasn't maintained an* interest in birds for years to come.

In real learning, the students are workers. And this learning needs to be measured by what students know and can do—by how well they can write or speak or calculate—not by how adept they are at picking out answers in a multiple-choice test. Understanding these facts about learning and assessment are the first steps to achieving the kind of curricula we need in restructured schools.

Quoted from "Forty Birds: Curriculum in the Restructured School" by Albert Shanker, president of the American Federation of Teachers, AFL-CIO. Reprinted with permission from *Cogitare: Newsletter of the ASCD Network on Teaching Thinking*, Vol. V (fall, 1990), 1, 3. Copyright by Association for Supervision and Curriculum Development.

Simply having students do science—by having them follow an experiment in cookbook fashion—will not lead to new understandings if their interest and intellect are not also engaged.

Children and Science: A Perfect Fit

Nobel laureate Rosalyn Yalow made the case for early science education for all children in a 1988 commencement address at Mt. Sinai Medical School in New York. "Taught properly, science can be part of the curriculum of the preschool as well as of the elementary school child," she said. "The teaching of science at this level does not require complicated, expensive apparatus. It *does* require a teacher imbued with a love for logical thinking and the imagination to design simple experimentation that permits the child to think of himself or herself as an investigator."[6]

which students made predictions, mapped patterns of plant growth, and offered explanations for what they were seeing. At the end of the unit, nine out of ten students failed to grasp the central concept: that plants get their food by manufacturing it internally out of carbon dioxide, water, and light energy.[7] They had gone through the motions of doing science but hadn't made the connection between their experiments and their understanding of the real world.

Children come to the classroom with many intuitive, everyday ways of explaining natural phenomena. Although these explanations may appear to be based on credible evidence, they are often wrong, as in the previous example, in which the students continued to conclude that plants draw their food up out of the ground. In such cases, students need to think about the purpose behind their "hands on" activities, to compare the actual results of their experiments with the predicted outcome. If there is a difference, what explains it? Experiential science succeeds when it causes students to abandon misconceptions and embrace scientifically valid principles. Consistent with modern learning theory, research shows that students who have the power to control some aspect of an experiment are much more likely to become fully engaged in interpreting the outcome than those who are simply asked to follow a protocol.

For Further Information

Bybee, Rodger, and others. *Science and Technology Education for the Elementary Years: Framework for Curriculum and Instruction.* Andover, Mass.: The National Center for Improving Science Education, 1989.

Getting Started in Science: A Blueprint for Elementary School Science. National Center for Improving Science Education. Andover, Mass.: The Network, Inc., 1989.

Levine, Joseph S. "Your Child Can Learn Science," *World Monitor*, (February, 1991), 40–46.

Loucks-Horsley, Susan, and others. *Elementary School Science for the 90s.* Alexandria, Va.: The Curriculum/Technology Resource Center, Association for Supervision and Curriculum Development, 1990.

Roth, Kathleen J. "Science Education: It's Not Enough to 'Do' or 'Relate,'" *American Educator,* Vol. 13 (Winter, 1989), 16–22, 46–48.

Science Framework for California Public Schools, Kindergarten Through Grade Twelve. Developed by the Science Curriculum Framework and Criteria Committee. Sacramento: California Department of Education, 1990.

Health Education and Physical Education in the Elementary Years

The health education and physical education curriculum helps students to know and practice good health habits that will last a lifetime. Health instruction should focus on health promotion, disease prevention, and risk reduction, with an emphasis on building social skills and self-esteem and guiding students toward appropriate decision making. The physical education program should help students develop motor skills and a knowledge of game and dance activities that build self-confidence and prepare them for an active adulthood while promoting cardiovascular development.

Certainly, the salient problem in health education and physical education at the elementary level is that, too often, they are allowed to become instructional afterthoughts. From a needs standpoint, this makes little sense. Children are less fit today than they were in the past. The number of children considered obese increased by 50 percent between 1963 and 1980, and the percent of severely overweight children in California's population, according to a recent study, is 40 percent greater than the national average.[8] Disturbing behavioral trends among adolescents—including the use of drugs, alcohol, and tobacco; unwanted pregnancies; sexually transmitted diseases; eating disorders; stress; and suicide—further underline the need for a renewed emphasis on the early prevention of threats to students' well-being.

In the past, common institutional response to self-destructive behaviors was to wait until the high school years to provide students with specific antismoking or antidrug programs. But such ad hoc programs were uniformly ineffective. Comprehensive health programs that enlist the cooperative efforts of school staff, parents, and the local community; that begin in elementary school; and that emphasize wise decision-making skills are a much better approach.

Developmentally appropriate physical education programs should be designed for every child, from the physically gifted to the physically challenged, to provide a foundation of movement experiences that give useful insights and lead to an active and healthy life-style. An exemplary

The salient problem in health education and physical education at the elementary level is that, too often, they are allowed to become instructional afterthoughts.

Fit Fifth Graders?

The 1989 and 1990 results of the *California Health-Related Fitness Test* reveal that fewer than one in five of the state's fifth graders can be considered physically fit. The test, based on standards developed by the American Alliance for Health, Physical Education, Recreation and Dance, consisted of five subtests: sit and reach, sit-ups, pull-ups, one-mile run/walk, and body composition. Standards for each subtest are based on a student's age and sex. Ten-year old boys, for example, are expected to complete the one-mile run/walk in 9 1/2 minutes, do 34 sit-ups in one minute, do one pull-up. Girls of the same age meet the minimum standards when they complete the mile in 11 minutes, do 30 sit-ups, and do one pull-up.

To be considered fit, a student has to meet at least 4 of the 5 fitness standards. The results of the 1990 testing of almost all the state's fifth-graders are displayed here.

Summary of Student Performance—1990
Percent of Students by Number of Standards Met

Students	4 or more standards	3	2	1	0
All	16	21	26	25	12
Boys	17	20	24	24	14
Girls	16	22	28	25	9

physical education curriculum provides a variety of continous, vigorous activities combined with less repetitive activities and may include a balance of games, dance, and educational gymnastics, resulting in enhanced skills and self-confidence. Children take part in scheduled, instructional activities in addition to daily recess time. Class activities deemphasize winning and losing and stress the importance of self-improvement and active participation.

Good health and safety habits begin early in life. Such practices as always wearing seat belts; knowing what to do if caught in a fire; being wary of the dangers of cigarettes, drugs, and alcohol; and enjoying the benefits of nutritious food and recreational exercise are valuable in themselves. The fact that they also have proved effective in protecting children against serious problems during adolescence is the single strongest argument for a coordinated health education and physical education program that begins in the elementary grades.

For Further Information

California Daily Food Guide: Dietary Guidance for Californians. Developed by the California Department of Health Services in collaboration with the California Department of Aging and the California Department of Education. Sacramento: California Department of Health Services, 1990.

Choose Well, Be Well: Nutrition Education Curriculum. Guides and resource manuals for preschool through grade twelve prepared by the Nutrition and Education Program, Office of Child Nutrition Services. Sacramento: California Department of Education, 1982–1985.

Handbook for Physical Education: Framework for Developing a Curriculum for California Public Schools, Kindergarten Through Grade Twelve. Developed by the Physical Education Handbook Committee, working in cooperation with the Physical Education and Athletics Unit, California Department of Education. Sacramento: California Department of Education, 1986.

Physical Best: The AAHPERD Guide to Physical Fitness Education and Assessment. Reston, Va.: The American Alliance for Health, Physical Education, Recreation, and Dance, 1989.

Second Languages in Elementary Years

Our national inability to speak other languages has been well documented and is becoming an increasing liability in the interdependent global marketplace. The establishment of sound second-language programs in California's elementary schools is an important step in overcoming our monolingualism.

Both research and experience demonstrate that a second language is best learned in a manner that approximates how the first language was acquired—by using the language to meet real needs. Thus, second-language programs in elementary schools should be designed on a communication-based approach—one which constantly relies on the language as the medium for the exchange of meaningful information and the communication of ideas.

Even though second-language instruction in the elementary years rebounded in California in the 1980s, a great deal of work remains to be done to approach the statewide goal of universal second-language acquisition. Less than 2 percent of the state's elementary students are enrolled in second-language classes; and in the majority of these classes, instruction is not given frequently enough nor for enough hours to make much of an impression.[9] This limited exposure is all the more regrettable because research shows that children are especially adept at picking up a new language in their unself-conscious preadolescence. And yet, most schools do not offer students second-language programs until students reach the ninth grade. Clearly, using what is developmentally appropriate as the

Second-language programs in elementary schools should be designed on a communication-based approach.

yardstick, a far greater emphasis on second-language programs in the elementary grades is urgently needed.

As matters stand, by far the largest and most successful second-language program in California's elementary grades is the effort to teach English to language-minority students. Almost every child who enters a kindergarten classroom not speaking English can expect to be a fluent English speaker by the end of the sixth grade. Too often, however, these programs permit command of the home language to dwindle as proficiency in English is acquired. This loss of precious linguistic resources is regrettable and contradicts the statewide goal that every student learn to communicate effectively in at least two languages.

In effective bilingual programs teachers develop the student's literacy skills in the home language before requiring the student to make the transition to English. Even after the student becomes proficient in English, the best of the state's bilingual programs continue to develop the student's home language. These programs help bond language-minority students and their families to the school, give students a valuable skill when they pursue higher education or enter the work force, and increase California's intellectual capital. These programs should be the rule rather than the exception.

Two-way language immersion is a program in which language-minority and language-majority students work together to become fully proficient in each others' languages. Typically, in California such programs feature instruction almost completely in Spanish beginning in kindergarten, with an incremental increase in English instruction in subsequent years. By the fifth grade, instructional time spent in English and Spanish reaches parity. The bilingual immersion model is equally valid in any second language, however. For example, the San Francisco Unified School District offers a two-way immersion program in Cantonese in the elementary grades.

Experience with two-way immersion has shown overwhelmingly positive effects from such programs. Speakers of English benefit by picking up a near-native command of a second language. Students new to English gain from the chance to build a strong literacy base in their home language, which enables them to succeed in the core curriculum. All students reach academic achievement levels equivalent to or better than their conventionally schooled grade-level peers.

For Further Information

Cummins, James. *Empowering Minority Students*. Sacramento: California Association for Bilingual Education, 1989.

Foreign Language Framework for California Public Schools, Kindergarten Through Grade Twelve. Developed by the Foreign Language Curriculum and Framework Committee. Sacramento: California Department of Education, 1989.

Logan, Gerald. *Handbook for Planning an Effective Foreign Language Program.*
    Sacramento: California Department of Education, 1985.
Studies on Immersion Education: A Collection for United States Educators.
    Prepared Under the Direction of the Office of Bilingual-Bicultural Education.
    Sacramento: California Department of Education, 1984.

Visual and Performing Arts in the Elementary Years

From the early years of elementary school, every California student should have access to a planned program in the visual and performing arts: dance, drama/theater, music, and the visual arts, including media arts. The *Visual and Performing Arts Framework* identifies four components of instruction: aesthetic perception, creative expression, arts heritage, and aesthetic valuing. The arts provide students a unique way of knowing about the world and themselves and communicating that knowledge and information. In a comprehensive arts program, students gain the skills necessary to express their ideas creatively. As they produce works in the arts, students have the opportunity to communicate in nonverbal ways. They study historical and contemporary arts from throughout the world and reflect on the role of the arts in many cultures. Students gain an increased awareness of and response to beauty in all its forms while they develop criteria to analyze, judge, and interpret works of art. They learn how to apply these standards to their own work and to improve the quality and beauty of their personal lives and the aesthetic environment of their community.

Arts instruction in the early grades affirms the natural joy children find in expressing themselves—in paint, in song, in dance, and in dramatic presentations. As they mature, their artistic energy and emerging creative ability can be promoted and enhanced by teaching the principles of drawing, how to read musical notation, the techniques of dance, and the craft of theater. Children should be afforded frequent opportunities to see professional arts performances, visit museums, and attend exhibits at school and in the community. Their critical powers can be honed by written reflection on what they hear and see. An exemplary elementary arts program includes both the doing and thinking about art. It includes self-expression, acquisition of skills, and a study of artistic traditions from many cultures.

The arts are studied in their own right as well as integrated in the child's history, literature, science, and foreign language lessons. Anyone who enters the schools sees, hears, and feels the presence of the arts through murals, exhibits, morning sings, and performances.

"The visual and performing arts offer students a language for exploring, creating, and expressing that helps develop self-esteem and communication with others and bridge cultural differences."

Susan Watts,
Kindergarten Teacher,
Benicia Unified School District

For Further Information

Handbook for Planning an Effective Visual and Performing Arts Program. Prepared by the County/State Steering Committee. Tulare, Calif.: Tulare County Office of Education, 1990.

Lehman, Paul R. "What Students Should Learn in the Arts," in *Content of the Curriculum*. 1988 Yearbook of the Association for Supervision and Curriculum Development. Alexandria, Va.: Association for Supervision and Curriculum Development, 1988.

Strengthening the Arts in California Schools: A Design for the Future. Developed by the Arts Education Advisory Committee. Sacramento: California Department of Education, 1990.

"Symposium: Arts as Education, Part I," *Harvard Educational Review*, Vol. 61 (February, 1991), 25–87.

Toward Civilization: A Report on Arts Education. Washington, D.C.: National Endowment for the Arts, 1988.

Visual and Performing Arts Framework for California Public Schools: Kindergarten Through Grade Twelve. Developed by the Curriculum Framework and Criteria Committee. Sacramento: California Department of Education, 1982, 1989.

Character Education in the Elementary Years

Character education is an essential part of the elementary schools' mission. It differs from other aspects of the thinking curriculum in significant ways, however. For one thing, it is not a separate domain within the curriculum but rather a vital strand running through each of the subject areas. For another, it is not a purely cerebral endeavor. Its goal is not simply to teach children about morality; it is to persuade and inspire them to be moral—to understand in their minds, embrace in their hearts, and act in their daily lives according to a pro-social set of values.

Character education takes place through both explicit and implicit means. Explicitly, the thinking curriculum in literature, science, history, and the other disciplines offers abundant opportunities to explore the moral dimensions of human behavior and inspire virtuous conduct. The great questions facing individuals and the human race are moral questions, and children, as seekers of meaning, are naturally drawn to thinking about and discussing them and how they bear on their own lives. Pro-social values are also encouraged implicitly—through the example of the school as a caring community. Everything that happens at school carries a message to children about what the adult world values and truly holds important. Schools that take moral education seriously consciously foster an atmosphere that respects and mutually supports students and staff. (See Chapter 5, "Creation of a Learning Environment").

Through most of this nation's history, the importance of moral instruction in the public schools was taken for granted. In the 1970s, however, a handful of critics challenged this bedrock assumption.[10] In a society as heterogeneous as our own, they argued, teaching children a single set of values amounted to oppression. In the face of this argument, many educators lost their confidence. It became common for classroom discussions to focus on eliciting the child's opinion as though questions of profound moral significance could be reduced to a matter of personal taste. Alternatively, teachers chose to avoid addressing issues of moral significance entirely.

The problem created by the teachers' diffidence regarding instruction in morals and values was that the school abdicated its traditional role as a transmitter of adult values essential to the survival and flourishing of our civilization. Furthermore, as many writers have observed, the attitude was based on the incorrect assumption that diversity in our society meant that a common set of values did not exist among us. As a matter of fact, however, just the opposite is true. Thomas Lickona writes that what enables us to co-exist despite our deep divisions over particular moral issues—abortion, euthanasia, and capital punishment, for instance—is a commitment to shared values.[11] Indeed, there are a host of personal character traits which people of good will, whatever their religious, ethnic, or cultural back-ground, overwhelmingly agree on as both good and desirable for their children to develop. These traits include honesty, civility, responsibility, tolerance, self-discipline, patience, compassion, reverence for life, pride in work, to name a few. Taken together, these qualities constitute our common ethical ground and are appropriate material for social bolstering in the elementary years.

Character education is not the sole responsibility of the schools. The primary influence on a child's moral formation is, and will always remain, what happens in the home. The point is, however, that parents need—and expect—all the support they can get in helping children become moral. Indeed, out of 25 possibilities listed on the Gallup Poll's annual survey of attitudes toward education in the U.S., the second highest show of approval generally is accorded the following goals for the public schools: "To develop standards of what is right and wrong." (Only the classic academic mission, "To develop the ability to speak and write correctly," consistently scores higher.)[12] Other institutions such as religious organizations and those that assist children in their moral and ethical development make important contributions to character education. However, beginning in the elementary years, schools have a special obligation to encourage children to adopt as their own the highest ethical standards of the community.

The great questions facing individuals and the human race are moral questions, and children, as seekers of meaning, are naturally drawn to thinking about and discussing them and how they bear on their own lives.

For Further Information

Grant, Gerald. "Schools That Make an Imprint: Creating a Strong Positive Ethos," in *Challenge to American Schools: The Case for Standards and Values.* Edited by John H. Bunzel. New York: Oxford University Press, 1985, pp. 127–143.

Moral and Civic Education and Teaching About Religion. Adopted by the California State Board of Education. Sacramento: California Department of Education, 1991.

Schaps, Eric, and Daniel Solomon. "Schools and Classrooms as Caring Communities," *Educational Leadership,* Vol. 48 (November, 1990), 38–42.

RECOMMENDATION

1

Make a rich, meaning-centered, thinking curriculum the centerpiece of instruction for all students in all subject areas in the elementary grades.

The Elementary Grades Task Force's portrait of an exemplary elementary curriculum may strike some as utopian. Admittedly, very few, if any, elementary schools in California are delivering every element of the educational program the Task Force has outlined. Readers should not be discouraged, however, by the ambitiousness of the vision summarized in Recommendation 1. As already noted, restructuring elementary schools to improve significantly the quality of education our children receive is a long-term process. The thinking curriculum won't become the norm overnight. In striving toward it, districts and schools will have to make choices that are sensible in terms of their own needs, priorities, and resources. However, we are not starting from scratch in this endeavor. California has already done much to identify policies and practices that will bring to life the changes contemplated here. Indeed, a main function of this report is to serve as a blueprint for change—to highlight successful initiatives and suggest how they might be more widely disseminated. The remainder of *It's Elementary!* deals with the questions of implementing the vision, beginning in Chapter 2, with what can be done in the classroom.

CHAPTER 2

IN THE CLASSROOM

THE CORE ELEMENTARY CURRICULUM CONTAINS A WEALTH OF IDEAS, insights, and powerful ways of knowing the world. All our children deserve the solid preparation for future schooling and success in their adult lives that such a curriculum promises. If one message was clear in the 26 regional hearings conducted by the Task Force, however, it was that elementary teachers embrace, but feel overwhelmed by, the extent of recent curricular change. After all, as several teachers and administrators correctly pointed out, middle school and high school teachers working within an academic discipline can concentrate on implementing powerful curriculum in one content area. But elementary teachers in self-contained classrooms have been deluged with new frameworks and model curriculum guides with the expectation that the new insights and strategies would be quickly assimilated, often with minimal help.

The purpose of this chapter of *It's Elementary!* is to provide some relief to teachers by identifying practical steps that can be taken in the classroom to speed the transition to the thinking curriculum. The recommendations of the Task Force for improving instructional practice are presented in three sections. The first two correspond to the questions skeptics ask most frequently about implementing the thinking curriculum. First, how will elementary teachers be able to implement such an ambitious program? And, second, how can they serve an increasingly diverse student population while doing so? The third section in this chapter focuses on the promise of technology in helping to support the thinking curriculum.

SECTION ONE

Fitting It All In

Teachers and elementary schools committed to making the transition to a rich, meaning-centered, thinking curriculum for all their students can budget their instructional time and gain better control of the change process by taking the steps proposed in recommendations 2 through 7.

RECOMMENDATION

2 Begin curricular reform by mastering a single subject area.

Teachers who are accustomed to using a skills-based curriculum should not be expected to shift overnight to one based on discovery. The best way to begin teaching the thinking curriculum is to focus efforts on one area of the curriculum. A teacher can study the appropriate framework, attend a summer staff development institute, or find a colleague who already has and can act as an informal adviser. Then, the teacher can begin trying out lessons consistent with the principles found in the framework. Because mathematics and language arts are central to the elementary curriculum,

A Teacher Speaks

There is just too much stuff for me to teach in a regular school day. I know everything is important but it's not humanly possible to do it all. Finally, someone (our mentor) had the foresight and planning process to look for big ideas and teach those. I'm doing only three units of science now (that's up from the one I halfheartedly taught two years ago), but I think I'll be able to handle the next two units soon. Funny thing is, if I had known how exciting this was, I would have done it a long time ago!

either one can provide a logical place to start. But *any* subject area can be considered because each of California's new generation of frameworks is based on a consistent philosophy of how children learn. Each calls for instructional strategies that involve students as active, engaged participants in their own learnings. In a very real sense, then, to master one framework is to gain insight into them all.

The transition to the thinking curriculum is a long-term project. The strategic advantage of picking a single area of the curriculum is that it makes an otherwise overwhelming task seem manageable. Once a beach-head of success has been established in one area, a teacher can apply the principles discovered there to the instructional strategies used to present the rest of the curriculum.

RECOMMENDATION

3 Reduce the amount of time spent on skill-based activities.

The thinking curriculum is not an add-on to the traditional curriculum. Rather, it represents a completely new approach in which less effective and time-consuming instructional practices are replaced by more stimulating ones. For example, daily spelling lessons from the traditional spelling book, organized around the tenuous rules of English spelling, can be eliminated in favor of more opportunities for writing in which students learn to spell the words they need to communicate their ideas. Similarly, time given to acquiring speed and skill in doing mathematical computations can be decreased in favor of giving students more time to solve real mathematical problems in which numbers are handled in context. And, of course, time now spent on stand-alone units of "critical thinking skills" can be set aside in favor of students actually thinking critically in the content areas.

RECOMMENDATION

4 Choose depth over coverage in teaching a subject.

Realistically, teaching a meaning-centered curriculum presupposes that the number of topics that are addressed in any given subject area is likely to decrease. The reason is simple: providing learning experiences in which the understanding of concepts is the goal takes more time than passing along bits and pieces of information. For example, it takes longer for students to develop an intriguing question in science, to design an experiment to find answers, to puzzle through the meaning of raw data, and to reconcile the findings with their original beliefs than it does to read a textbook and answer the ubiquitous questions at the end of a chapter. On

"Because the learner is constantly searching for connections on many levels, educators need to orchestrate the experiences from which learners extract understanding. They must do more than simply provide information or force the memorization of isolated facts and skills."

Renate N. Caine and Geoffrey Caine[1]

"Out With the Old, In With the New"

In its landmark publication, *Curriculum and Evaluation Standards for School Mathematics*, the National Council of Teachers of Mathematics has called for a dramatic change in the mathematics curriculum most elementary students experience. If students are to become mathematical problem solvers, they must experience a curriculum that provides opportunities to be active participants in creating knowledge rather than always being treated as passive rule followers. To this end, the NCTM standards suggest specific areas of the curriculum for *increased* attention: solving everyday problems, using estimation to determine the reasonableness of answers, using manipulative materials and writing about mathematics. Other areas of the curriculum should receive *decreased* attention: long division, rote memorization of rules, worksheets, and identifying clue words to determine which operation to use in problem solving.[2]

the other hand, activity-based instruction also gives students a vastly more robust insight into how science works. And it provides learnings that students are far more likely to retain. There will always be a need to balance the competing claims of depth versus breadth of coverage in any subject area. But experience shows, and the advice of the Task Force in this regard is clear, less is more. A handful of profound learning experiences is more educationally valuable than skimming reams of information superficially.

RECOMMENDATION

5 **Schedule class work in longer blocks of time.**

A thinking curriculum in which students gain deep understandings requires changes in the way time is scheduled in the elementary schools. The traditional skills-based curriculum lent itself to short blocks of time for each subject area. Students were introduced to a narrowly defined skill by a teacher, provided with some directed practice in its mastery, and then given worksheets to be done independently either in school or at home. But the thinking curriculum requires longer blocks of time—extending over not just several hours but over days or even weeks of effort. For example, 45 minutes is seldom enough time to identify a problem, look for a pattern, play with competing solutions, and write up a comprehensive explanation in mathematics. An hour is not sufficient time to write and publish a class newsletter.

One of the natural consequences of pursuing authentic learning tasks over longer blocks of time is that this approach tends to dissolve the rigid distinctions between subject areas. For instance, fifth grade students who read *If You Traveled West in a Covered Wagon* by Ellen Levine and then write their own pretend-diary as if they were participating in such a journey are acquiring deep historical knowledge as well as honing their language arts skills. In a health lesson about the importance of getting enough sleep, students might make a graph of their classmates' various bedtimes and, while so engaged, discuss some important mathematical issues, such as sources of error in data collection.

Good interdisciplinary instruction has a place in the thinking curriculum. To carry it off successfully, however, teachers need to have a clear vision of what they are trying to accomplish in each content area that day, week, month, and year—lest the rigor of the individual subject areas be lost. As a bridge into this world, teachers might try creating a two discipline unit in naturally related subjects such as mathematics and science. Integrating units has the benefit of sanctioning lessons that last up to two hours, enough time for students to really get something accomplished.

RECOMMENDATION

6 **Team teach and specialize, especially in the upper elementary grades.**

Even with the best of intentions, elementary teachers will find themselves frustrated in trying to deliver the thinking curriculum unless they start with a solid working knowledge of the subject areas they are charged with helping students explore. Professional development to enhance teachers' knowledge is so critical to improving elementary education that it is the focus of its own chapter in this report. In the meantime, however, schools can follow certain effective strategies to take advantage of the strengths of their faculties and save teachers' preparation time. These include various forms of team teaching and specialization:

1. Teachers in a given grade level might divide the subject area domains among themselves, based on their own assessment of their particular abilities, professional experience, and interests. They then rotate through the various classrooms at a given grade level, teaching the same activity-based lesson plan.

2. School districts might elect to employ teachers with special expertise and use their talents at the school sites. Or districts may choose to bring in guest teachers for a few periods a day or a few days a week.

3. The "lead teacher" concept is another powerful spur to schoolwide professional growth. A lead teacher is designated in each subject area at each grade level. In addition to keeping abreast of develop-

ments in their chosen field and sharing this information with their colleagues, lead teachers work with the principal to design curricula, select instructional materials, and coach their colleagues as they implement new approaches in classrooms. Often these individuals are alumni of summer training institutes in their respective disciplines and serve as teacher representatives to district curriculum committees.

In kindergarten through grade three, young children need the reassurance of a homeroom teacher who is present in loco parentis for most of the day. In grades four through six, however, more flexibility is possible. Schools can begin to experiment in the upper elementary grades with limited degrees of departmentalizing the instructional day. Thus, a teacher particularly adept at provoking discussions of text might present a unit in literature to several classes while the lead teacher in science might present a hands-on science unit at the same time on an exchange basis. Once again, the overall strategy should be to lead from strength—to divide the workload so that teachers end up spending most of their time in those subject areas they particularly enjoy teaching and in which they feel most competent.

RECOMMENDATION

7 Extend the learning day with homework assignments consistent with the thinking curriculum.

Homework is an effective and inexpensive way to increase instructional time and, thus, an essential aid in helping teachers working with the thinking curriculum "fit it all in." As has traditionally been the case, skills that are necessary for academic achievement may be practiced away from school. This use of homework frees up classroom time for other activities. While practice is useful, however, a new, more creative view of homework is emerging. Homework assignments can (1) prepare students for upcoming lessons (by asking them to gather data, attempt solutions to complex problems, write rough drafts, do background reading, or otherwise provide a strong basis for in-class learning activities); (2) extend classroom learnings (by transferring them to situations in the child's home environment); and (3) create new understandings (by calling on students to create original work products that integrate or synthesize diverse skills or concepts). All students in the elementary grades should be assigned, on a regular basis, homework that piques their curiosity, taps their inventiveness, and engages them in a variety of unpredictable learning adventures consistent with the thinking curriculum.

Research shows that homework has the best effect on student achievement when children receive feedback on what they have done. Homework should never be assigned, handed in, and forgotten; rather, it should serve as a springboard for classroom activities and discussions. The best homework assignments do not require students to find the "one right answer." Rather, they invite students to find original solutions. For example, students might be asked to answer this question: How far is it around the block where you live? One child might attack the question by pacing off the distance. Another might measure the number of lengths with a garden hose. Still another might clip a card to a bicycle tire, counting the clicks that occur and multiply them times the tire's circumference. All students should be given opportunities to discuss how they arrived at their solutions and compare the advantages of their different strategies. Such activities reinforce the notion that there are multiple pathways to a given intellectual destination. They also demonstrate that learning occurs everywhere—not just in the classroom—and that it is a lifelong endeavor.

While schools can count on most caregivers to eagerly support a well-conceived homework program, socioeconomic pressures have resulted in an increasing number of children who no longer enjoy this advantage. In those instances, the proper response from a school or school district is not to give up on the idea of homework; rather, it is to set up alternative programs to foster after-class involvement—through the formation of peer study groups; community homework centers staffed with older students, community volunteers, parents, and educators; and through homework call-in lines or panel programs on local cable television. Chapter 1 of the Education Consolidation and Improvement Act (ECIA) or the School Improvement Program (SIP) are tailor-made to provide the modest amounts of money needed to start such support programs.

How much homework should elementary students be expected to do per night or per week? An underlying assumption of the thinking curricula

All students in the elementary grades should be assigned, on a regular basis, homework that piques their curiosity, taps their inventiveness, and engages them in a variety of unpredictable learning adventures.

What Did You Do In School Today?

A new technological wrinkle with a big payoff has been installed at Los Naranjos Elementary School in Irvine, California: a voice mail system which allows parents to call in, enter a numerical code, and hear their children's teachers tell them what was taught in class that day, what parents can do to further the lesson, and what homework their children are expected to complete. As an added benefit, messages can be programmed in many languages, making the school more approachable to parents who don't speak English. On a typical school night, half the school's parents call in to retrieve the teachers' messages. Teachers report that homework completion rates have gone way up and students are coming to school better prepared.

is that learning requires hard work. As a rule, children in the United States are asked to do much less homework than their international peers. In answering the time-on-homework question, teachers must use their professional judgment. Clearly, the nature of the assignments themselves has an impact on how much time is appropriate. Homework that involves active explorations and includes peer or family participation provides an entirely different experience from assignments that focus on repetitious drills. It would be inappropriate, for example, to ask a first- or second-grade child to do an hour's worth of computational exercises, but an assignment to go to the store with mom or dad and help read and compare prices, add up the cost of items, count change, and so on could easily take an hour or longer but be entirely appropriate.

For Further Information

Cooper, Harris. *Homework: Research on Teaching Monograph.* New York: Longman, 1989.

Cooper, Harris M. "Synthesis of Research on Homework," *Educational Leadership*, Vol. 47 (November, 1989), 85–91.

Thomas, John W., and William D. Rohwer, Jr. "Academic Studying: The Role of Learning Strategies," *Educational Psychologist*, Vol. 21 (Winter/Spring, 1986), 19–41.

SECTION TWO

Taking Advantage of Diversity

The seeds of success or failure in school are planted early. By the third or fourth grade, it is possible to forecast with disconcerting accuracy which students will move swimmingly through the remainder of their public education and which ones will drop out before earning their high school diploma. Past realities need not dictate future trends, however. All children can learn and, more specifically, all can benefit from participating in a powerful thinking curriculum that energizes all segments of the student population. Numerous schools in California have had outstanding success working with students who, according to conventional wisdom, should not have fared well in their education. Too often, the so-called "risk factors" become self-fulfilling prophecies of failure: low income, limited-English proficiency, minority status, learning disabilities, low parent educational level, poor attendance, family upheaval, early reading difficulties, and so on. The fact is, the quality of the instructional program and expectations of the staff influence mightily the child's learning. The purpose of this section of *It's Elementary!* is to identify instructional practices that help ensure the success of all students.

RECOMMENDATION

8 **Use a variety of grouping strategies.**

The use of a variety of classroom grouping strategies helps guarantee that all students gain access to a rich, meaning-centered curriculum. Specifically, in the course of any given day, a student should move through a succession of work constellations designed by the teacher for whole class, individual, and small group settings. The particular grouping strategy used at any given moment will depend on the specific learning goal at hand.

Whole class grouping has fallen into disrepute of late because of its association with a lecture-centered pedagogy in which students are forced into a too passive learning role. The fact is, however, that there are many activities for which the whole group setting is an appropriate instructional choice—"setting the table" for small group or individual activities, consensus-building in the class, and conducting summary discussions, for example. Even a critical function of the teacher—making public the thinking processes that an expert uses in reading a text, writing an essay, solving a problem in mathematics, science, or other discipline—can be usefully carried out in the whole class setting.

It is not the whole group setting itself, in other words, but how the teacher is conducting a class that determines whether the aims of the thinking curriculum are being served. When a teacher gives undivided attention to one student, the rest of the class is left unattended. Because

Grouping and the Thinking Curriculum

A skills-based curriculum tends to dictate homogeneous class groupings with all the disadvantages that strategy entails. After all, in order for an assembly line to function properly, everyone must work at the same speed. But the thinking curriculum lends itself to heterogeneous groupings because encouraging students to think for themselves, by its very nature, means countenancing learning at different speeds and in different directions. As UCLA's Jeannie Oakes has noted, "Heterogeneous groups of students . . . do best in classrooms where the curriculum content is challenging, complex, related to real life, and—most of all—rich with meaning." When learning tasks are active rather than passive, when they are full of complications that require multiple abilities (thinking, discussing, writing, visualizing) rather than simple answers; when they are modeled on complex and challenging real world problem solving; when students are encouraged to work on them together rather than alone, Oakes writes, "the range of skill differences among students . . . diminish[es] greatly as an obstacle to teaching and learning."[3]

whole class instruction maximizes the number of students who benefit from contact with the teacher, artfully conducted whole group instruction remains an important tool in the classroom armamentarium.

Small groups, because they multiply the opportunities for students to take control of their own learnings, are a natural fit with the thinking curriculum. They can be organized to fit into a number of criteria and to serve a number of purposes. Small groups can be formed by (1) learning activity (for example, reciprocal reading groups of two to seven students take turns asking questions, summarizing, making predictions about, and clarifying a text); (2) personality type (for example, sometimes the teacher may want to team less assertive children together to give them a chance to "take over" the learning process); (3) social pattern (for example, sometimes it may be necessary to break up a group of boisterous pals or desirable to broaden contacts among students); (4) common interest; (5) random association; (6) ability in a given academic skill; or (7) the duration of a work project.

Whole Group Instruction Reconsidered

Although the number of children in Asian math classes is significantly greater than the number in American classes, Asian students receive much more teacher-led instruction than American students do. In Taiwan, the teacher was the leader of the child's activity 90 percent of the time in the classes we observed, as opposed to 74 percent in Japan and only 46 percent in the United States. The critical factor in this erosion of instructional time was the substantial amount of time American teachers spent with individuals or small groups. The problem is, when teachers provide individual instruction during normal class hours, they must leave the rest of the class unattended and, thus, the instructional time for all remaining children is reduced.

Whole-class instruction in the U.S. has gotten a somewhat bad reputation. It has become associated with too much talk and too many passive, tuned-out students. But, as we found in our observations of Asian classrooms, whole-class instruction in Japan and China is a very lively, engaging enterprise. Asian teachers do not spend large amounts of time lecturing. They present interesting problems to the whole class; they pose provocative questions; they probe and guide. The students work hard generating multiple approaches to a solution, explaining the rationale behind their methods and making good use of wrong answers.

How do Asian teachers handle diversity in students' knowledge and skills in the whole-group setting? Tracking does not exist in Asian

The grouping of students of similar academic abilities as the main organizing strategy for mathematics and English/language arts instruction remains too common in many elementary schools. Typically, these schools use a variety of criteria to assign students to classrooms but then regroup them by perceived achievement levels during specific instructional periods. In theory, the advantage of this within-class homogenous grouping is that it helps teachers tailor instruction to the students' needs. That is, by effectively reducing the diversity within the instructional group, teachers make it possible to provide instruction that is neither too easy nor too hard for most students.

Unfortunately, the dangers from an overreliance on ability grouping are manifold. For one thing, ability grouping tends to breed a culture of failure and behavioral contagion among students placed in low-achieving groups—that is, students who are always in an atmosphere of failure act out their frustrations over their lack of success. However euphemistically these groups may be named, the low-achieving students know who they are and

elementary schools—not for reading instruction, for math instruction nor by classroom according to presumed levels of intellectual ability. Instead, teachers use a variety of approaches that allows students who do not understand one approach to an idea to encounter the material in other ways. Discussion alternates with periods in which children work with concrete materials or struggle in small groups to come up with their own solutions.

American schools have attempted to cope with diversity by segregating children into different groups and spending large amounts of regular class time working with individuals. The unintended result of this strategy is that most American children—even first graders—receive teacher-led instruction less than half the time during mathematics classes. Asian teachers, on the other hand, have focused on the perfection of the whole-group lesson in the belief that, if done well, it can be made to work for every child. Asian teachers operate on what would be considered in the West a "constructivist" view of learning—but do so in the whole-class setting. What the Japanese and Chinese examples demonstrate so compellingly is that when widely implemented, such practices can produce extraordinary outcomes.

Adapted from "How Asian Teachers Polish Each Lesson to Perfection" by James W. Stigler and Harold W. Stevenson. Reprinted with permission from the spring, 1991 issue of the *American Educator*, the quarterly journal of the American Federation of Teachers, pp. 17–20, 45.

tend to perform well below their capabilities as they behave in conformity to perceived adult expectations. The problem is widespread. Even well-regarded schools make the mistake of withholding a rigorous curriculum from students stuck in low-ability groups. Instead, these children get endless sessions of drilling the basics. Clearly, if students spend the reading hour filling in skill sheets instead of listening to and discussing interesting reading selections, the gap that exists in active language mastery and comprehension skills between them and their high-achieving peers will only increase. A heartbreaking outcome of rigid ability grouping is that perfectly able children whose learning aptitudes were misdiagnosed in the first place can become marooned in a "dumbed-down" instructional setting, with no way back to the thinking curriculum. Finally, as an ethical matter, the extensive use of ability grouping tends to increase divisions along class, race, and ethnic lines and, hence, is incompatible with our society's democratic ideals.

How, then, should a teacher proceed when confronted with a classroom full of young students endowed with a broad spectrum of language abilities and learning backgrounds? The answer: Stay flexible in classroom management practices. Use the grouping strategy best suited to the specific learning goal at hand. And keep it temporary. Groups should be periodically created, modified, or disbanded as new learning needs arise. Ability grouping in limited doses is an acceptable instructional practice. However, it must be the exception in the child's instructional day, not the rule. In the elementary years, the child's primary identification as a student should remain in the homeroom class, with most of the day spent in a variety of instructional settings.

For Further Information

Oakes, Jeannie, and Martin Lipton. *Making the Best of Schools: A Handbook for Parents, Teachers, and Policymakers.* New Haven:Yale University Press, 1990.

Slavin, Robert E. "Ability Grouping and Student Achievement in Elementary Schools: A Best-Evidenced Synthesis," *Review of Education Research*, Vol. 57 (Fall, 1987), 293–336.

RECOMMENDATION

9 Provide more collaborative learning opportunities.

Children of different academic levels often derive benefits from working together in small groups to reach common learning goals. This model for organizing children for classroom activities, known as cooperative or collaborative learning, has certain inherent advantages over simply having students work in groups. It more closely resembles how humans work in the real world and, therefore, promotes the development of social skills. (Only in school, Lauren Resnick writes, are humans customarily required to work in isolation.[4]) It provides opportunities for children to be actively involved in the learning process and assume responsibility for their own intellectual excursions. And it can be used as an alternative to within-class grouping.

Why does collaborative learning work? Students benefit from their involvement in well-run collaborative groups because they can watch—and learn from—the way classmates attack new learning tasks. Each child brings a unique set of experiences, perspectives, and world views to the collaborative learning group that can both enrich and be enriched by contact

A Cooperative Math Lesson in Logical Thinking

Children in a second-grade classroom are clustered in cooperative groups of four. Their assignment is to solve several math "thought" problems collaboratively. At one table, three of the students are kneeling on their chairs, "putting their heads together." Javier, the only fully seated child and the group's "recorder," is laboriously printing an answer on the group's single answer sheet. The group members look on quietly as he finishes.

Rachel: (The group's facilitator.) "Okay, what's next?"
Susan: (The reader.) "Portia and Freddy bought a pizza.
            The man cut it into eight pieces. 'Would you cut it into 16
            pieces, please?' asked Portia. 'We are really hungry.' Would
            cutting the pizza into 16 pieces help?"
Javier: "It's the same! It's still the same!"
Susan: "Yeah. Because the pizza doesn't grow. That's stupid."
Rachel: "What's the same?"
Javier: "The pizza is still the same. There isn't any more if you make
            16 pieces."
Susan: "But the pieces will be smaller."
Rachel: "Oh, yeah. Right. They don't get any more."
Toby: (The checker.) "Does everyone agree?"
            Everyone nods and Javier starts to write the group answer:
            "No, because the pieces will be smaller."
            "Good thinking!" Rachel concludes.

Successful interactions like this don't happen automatically. Cooperative learning looks deceptively easy when it works, but the teacher has set the stage by cultivating a climate of respect and concern for others, by observing previous group interactions, by assigning roles to group members and by a judicious selection of learning tasks.

Adapted from "A Cooperative Mathematics Lesson in Logical Thinking." Reprinted with permission from the winter, 1988, issue of *Working Together*, published by The Child Development Project, p. 9.

with others. Furthermore, the very process of working together to attain a common goal fosters pro-social values. By sharing materials, taking turns, or deciding how to settle a difference of opinion, children learn the importance of fairness. By listening to the person talking or learning how to make suggestions without being bossy, they show concern and respect for others. By putting forth effort for the good of the group, they show responsibility.

The expanded use of collaborative learning is an important adjunct in the education of California's elementary students. It is not a panacea, however. Robert Slavin, one of the foremost advocates of the approach, worries that teachers will interpret collaborative learning to mean that students can be placed in groups, given materials or an interesting problem to solve, and then turned loose to discover what they will. Such an approach is a prescription for disaster. Students must be taught the skills of cooperative behavior; they are not innate. Nor will they be ready to assume complete responsibility for their own learning overnight. "Successful models always include plain old good instruction," Slavin sums up the issue. "The cooperative activities supplement but do not replace direct instruction. What they *do* replace is individual seatwork."[5]

For Further Information

Caine, Renate N., and Geoffrey Caine. *Making Connections: Teaching and the Human Brain*. Alexandria, Va.: Association for Supervision and Curriculum Development, 1991.

"Cooperative Learning," *Educational Leadership*, Vol. 47 (December, 1989/ January, 1990), 4–15.

Johnson, David W., and Roger T. Johnson. *Learning Together and Alone: Cooperative, Competitive, and Individualistic Learning*. Englewood Cliffs, N.J.: Prentice-Hall, Inc., 1991.

Johnson, David W., and others. *Circles of Learning. Cooperation in the Classroom*. Edina, Minn.: Interaction Book Co., 1990.

Kohn, Alfie. "P Is for Prosocial Teaching," *The Boston Globe Magazine*, November 6, 1988.

Watson, Marilyn S.; Carolyn Hildebrandt; and Daniel Solomon. "Cooperative Learning as a Means of Promoting Pro-social Development Among Kindergarten and Early Primary-Grade Children," *International Journal of Social Education*, Vol. 3 (Fall, 1988), 34–47.

RECOMMENDATION

10 **Intervene early to prevent learning problems, especially in reading fluency.**

"An ounce of prevention is worth a pound of cure," as Poor Richard put it. In elementary education, however, an ounce of prevention may well be worth a lifetime of social usefulness because this is the stage in a child's

Teaching Reading Self-Sufficiency

The Reading Recovery teacher listens as the child begins by rereading easy books. The teacher suggests, "Read it with your finger."

"Now it comes out right," the child replies, "I had enough words for each time I pointed."

The teacher offers no assistance as the child rereads the book they worked on together during the previous lesson. They continue with the lesson until the child stops, puzzled.

"That didn't make any sense," the child observes, repeating the beginning of the sentence, taking another look. Then, after a moment, the child reflects aloud, "Oh, it's *away*. That makes sense."

A little later, the child shakes her head and seems uncertain. The teacher asks, "Why did you stop?"

"I don't remember that word."

"What word would make sense there?"

"*Bike*. But this word is longer. It's got to be bike. Oh! It's *bicycle*!"

By asking questions, the teacher helps the child correct her own errors. The teacher does not ask the child to "sound out the word" because this interrupts meaning processing. The teacher does not tell the word to the child, a procedure that tends to keep the child dependent upon the adult.

Quoted from "Reading Intervention for High-Risk First-Graders" by Mary Boehnlein. Reprinted with approval from the March, 1987 issue of *Educational Leadership*, p. 35. Copyright by Association for Supervision and Curriculum Development.

development when learning problems are still small enough to be overcome. The indispensable link in a prevention-oriented strategy of helping students before they acquire a self-image of academic failure is an aggressive program of literacy promotion. Reading is fundamental to most academic learning. Not surprisingly, the ability to read is highly predictive of future school success. In fact, a child's reading fluency at the third grade level gives a more accurate forecast of whether he or she will drop out or graduate from high school than any other indicator.

Research pioneered by Marie Clay in New Zealand led to her development of the Reading Recovery Program that is now being implemented in 22 states, including California. It is an example of a highly effective way to help struggling young readers catch up with their classmates through a carefully orchestrated program of one-on-one tutoring.

Details of effective early interventions like Reading Recovery vary from program to program, but the essential elements of successful programs include:

A child's reading fluency at the third grade level gives a more accurate forecast of whether he or she will drop out or graduate from high school than any other indicator.

1. They begin early (in the first grade, before children have begun to think of themselves as academic incompetents).
2. They provide daily, intensive one-on-one practice sessions of 20 minutes to a half hour over a 15 to 20 week period.
3. They are conducted by a specially trained teacher who knows how to observe and record children's literacy development and to tailor instruction specifically to the child's needs.

The goal of an early intervention reading program is to build the child's confidence in being able to read independently. Thus, in practice sessions, self-correction rather than a teacher's correction is emphasized. The student is always the active performer in each learning encounter. Through careful coaching, the teacher models and reinforces basic assumptions about text as well as an array of strategies for eliciting meaning when the child gets stuck. For example, the child learns that you can guess at words in context; you can use clues from the pictures; you can draw on background knowledge; you can reread and take a self-corrective action;

Cross-age Tutoring: a Two-way Street

The meta-analysis of cross-age tutoring programs indicates that all students involved in the program benefit in their attitudes toward school and learning—both the younger students who are read to and the older ones who do the reading. Jeff, a fifth-grade student with an average IQ, had been labeled an unmotivated underachiever by previous teachers. He would turn in half-completed assignments. His monotone oral reading was slow and hesitant, a possible indication he was not attending to the meaning. Jeff entered the cross-age reading program in his typical, lethargic way.

Jeff began to show interest in reading about two weeks into the program when he found a book that genuinely interested him. His appreciation of the story, *Noisy Nora*, was apparent by the fact that he shared a similar, personal experience with the kindergarten student to whom he was reading. As the program continued, Jeff began to read more books on a voluntary basis—and became more involved in other aspects of school. His science teacher noted that Jeff was showing a new willingness to take risks and participate in class. By the end of the school year, Jeff had read and reported on 45 books and his teachers voted him "Most Improved Student of the Year."

Adapted from "Cross-Age Reading: A Strategy for Helping Poor Readers," by Linda D. Labbo and William H. Teale. Reprinted with approval from the February, 1990, issue of *The Reading Teacher*©, pp. 362, 368.

you can go on without knowing every word. Contrast this set of options with the only two reading strategies most low-achieving readers can name: "I try to sound it out," they say. Or, "I ask the teacher."

Early intervention programs in reading are expensive in the short run, but they are cost-effective in the long run because they work—and keep on working. Coaching the very lowest achieving first grade students, Marie Clay in New Zealand and researchers in Ohio found that between 70 and 90 percent of those who were tutored caught up with their classmates. Furthermore, in follow-up studies four or five years later, these children were continuing to function without further help at levels comparable to their age-group peers.[6] In other words, once "slow" students gain a grip on how to read for meaning, they never need reading remediation again. Plus, they are able to continue profiting from regular classroom instruction—at a tremendous cumulative system-wide savings in time, money, and resources. Investing in the primary years in making sure every student learns how to read is ultimately both kinder and less expensive than sponsoring a parallel track for failing students in the intermediate, middle grade, and high school years.

For Further Information

Clay, Marie M. *The Early Detection of Reading Difficulties* (Third edition). Portsmouth, N.H.: Heinemann, 1985.

Pinnell, G. S. "Success for Low Achievers Through Reading Recovery," *Educational Leadership*, Vol. 48 (September, 1990), 17–21.

Pinnell, G. S.; M. Fried; and R. Estice. "Reading Recovery: Learning How to Make a Difference," *The Reading Teacher,* Vol. 43 (January, 1990), 282–295.

Slavin, Robert E., and Nancy A. Madden. "What Works for Students at Risk: A Research Synthesis," *Educational Leadership*, Vol. 46 (February, 1989), 4–13.

RECOMMENDATION

11 **Develop an academic support network to ensure that all students acquire important learnings the first time around.**

Not all children learn at the same rate. Some require more time than others to catch on to key concepts in certain instructional areas. Good teachers are sensitive to these differences and find ways to make sure their children receive the extra attention and time on task that their learning processes may require. With 30 children or more in a typical elementary classroom in California, how can this extra attention be provided? Several strategies, which can be funded through Chapter 1 of the ECIA or other categorical resources, present themselves:

1. By staggering the school day to allow some students to arrive before or leave after others, pupil-teacher ratios can be reduced during parts of the day, which would open the way for more direct teacher contact with students.

2. As more schools move to year-round scheduling, intersession classes for students in need of extra attention are possible.

3. Community involvement is a valuable source of extra help in the instructional program. Parents, college students, retired adults, and other volunteers can tutor, guide, and support students who need additional assistance.

4. Instructional time can be extended by providing extra classes before school, after school, and on Saturdays.

5. Children can teach each other, too. Homework cooperatives provide opportunities for students to coach one another through difficult assignments. Peer-tutoring and cross-age tutoring programs generate mutually beneficial experiences for children on both sides of the learning equation. For example, a San Antonio, Texas, cross-age tutoring program has been credited with helping decrease the drop-out rate among older Hispanic students by making them feel needed within the school system again.

For Further Information

Every Student Succeeds: A California Initiative to Ensure Success for Students at Risk. Sacramento: California Department of Education, 1990.

Labbo, Linda D., and William H. Teale. "Cross-Age Reading: A Strategy For Helping Poor Readers," *The Reading Teacher*, Vol. 48 (February, 1990), 362–369.

Slavin, Robert E. and others. *Effective Programs for Students at Risk*. Boston: Allyn and Bacon, Inc., 1989.

RECOMMENDATION

12 Use categorical resources to support the thinking curriculum.

Categorical programs were created to give help toward mastery of the core curriculum to children of poverty, the gifted and talented, the limited-English-proficient, and others with exceptional learning needs, abilities, or requirements. Collectively, these programs represent a sizable amount of money that can be used to support the academic success of target students.

The history of categorical programs is one of good intentions, major expenditures, and mixed results. Beginning in the 1960s, state and federal legislators, concerned that certain groups of students were not thriving in the public schools, began setting aside special funds to address their needs. Before long, a group of categorical programs had been enfranchised—

Chapter 1, migrant education, special education, bilingual education, gifted and talented education, school improvement, Chapter 2, SB 1882. Often, when new monies from these initiatives reached the school site, they were turned into new instructional programs—complete with their own staffs, space, internal culture, and curricula.

The central weakness of unsuccessful categorical programs was that they frequently shortchanged their students. Too often, the various programs tended to supplant the school district's core curriculum with a less intellectually nourishing one. As the number and scope of categorical programs increased, many districts realized they no longer had a core curriculum, but rather, any number of stand-alone alternatives.

The key, then, to helping children with special learning needs prosper in school is to have categorical funds support the core curriculum rather than pay for intellectually impoverished alternatives for several target groups. Although specific requirements pertaining to the use of categorical funds need to be observed, new flexibilities in the laws encourage and reward schools for using innovative strategies that hold the promise of educational success for all children. For example, many California school districts are already investing their categorical resources in the mainstream classroom instead of in "pull-out" programs. Furthermore, most categorical programs encourage the allocation of time and resources for coordination with the regular program. Thus, staff development funds may be used to support training activities for all staff who work with the targeted students, not just the staff who are paid with categorical programs funds. An intensive staff development program aimed at reforming the school's mathematics program, including money for released time and follow-up, could be mounted for about the same cost as one instructional aide's annual salary. But the schoolwide benefits to students from improved instruction would be incomparably greater.

In many cases existing categorical monies can be tapped to pay for the improvement initiatives recommended in this section—setting up early intervention programs, developing a cross-age tutoring program, or establishing Saturday classes, for example.

All of this, of course, implies a bold departure from the way things have long been done. Many school leaders believe they have no money to pay for school improvement strategies because their discretionary funds associated with categorical programs are spent as staff salaries before the school year begins. The solution, of course, is to have fewer categorical staff and more investment in systemic improvement.

For Further Information

Adamson, David R.; Judy Cox; and Joan Schuller. "Collaboration/Consultation: Bridging the Gap from Resource Room to Regular Classroom," *Teacher Education and Special Education*, Vol. 12 (Winter/Spring, 1989), 52–55.

RECOMMENDATION

13 **Ensure that limited-English-proficient (LEP) students have access to the thinking curriculum.**

Limited-English-proficient students composed 29 percent of the entering kindergarten class of 1990 in California.[7] Obviously, California's elementary schools must find ways to deliver the thinking curriculum to this large and growing segment of the student population.

In those cases where large numbers of LEP students have the same home language, the Elementary Grades Task Force recommends that classes be conducted in the LEP child's home language. This includes classes of instruction in initial literacy. An impressive body of research supports this recommendation. Learning to read in the home language is the fastest and most efficient way the LEP child can acquire English reading skills because children efficiently transfer to the second language the underlying principles of literacy they learn in their home language. Content-based primary language instruction combined with a regular program of English language development for LEP students is being used by an increasing number of elementary schools in the state with impressive results.

However, many of our elementary schools enroll only a few LEP students or several LEP students from different language groups. Providing

Student Study Teams

One of the most effective ways a school can demonstrate its commitment to pupils who are encountering problems in the regular program is by means of Student Study Teams (SSTs). SSTs usually consist of the referring teacher, school principal, parents of the student, and any resource person with an expertise in the problem area—ranging from the school reading specialist, bilingual specialist or counselor to the nurse or community service liaison. In grades four through six, the student also takes part in SST meetings. The purpose of the meetings is to draw on the knowledge of the assembled braintrust to develop an action plan—with agreed-on benchmarks—for increasing the student's success in school. One of the first California districts to experiment in this area, the Mt. Diablo School District, found that SSTs led to a reduction by half in referrals to its special education programs. More students were able to remain in the regular classroom and progress at a satisfactory rate. Regular classroom teachers received the help they needed. Parent cooperation was excellent, and the program contributed to a significant improvement in home-school climate in the district.

home language instruction in these instances is often difficult. Nonetheless, schools still have the responsibility of making sure that LEP children have access to a rich instructional program. This access can be provided through a variety of techniques, including modifying the way English is used in the classroom, grouping students to ensure that LEP pupils have access to bilingual peers, making available home language instructional materials, and connecting instruction to students' life experiences.

For Further Information

Bilingual Education Handbook: Designing Instruction for LEP Students. Sacramento: California Department of Education, 1990.

Cummins, James. "The Role of Primary Language Development in Promoting Educational Success for Language Minority Students," in *Schooling and Language Minority Students: A Theoretical Framework.* Los Angeles: Evaluation, Dissemination, and Assessment Center, California State University, 1981.

Krashen, Stephen, and Douglas Biber. *On Course: Bilingual Education's Success in California.* Sacramento: California Association for Bilingual Education, 1988.

RECOMMENDATION

14 **Avoid grade-level retention as an instructional strategy.**

Having sketched some of the most effective ways to include all students in the thinking curriculum, the Task Force also believes a few words should be said about what manifestly does *not* work. A common strategy for dealing with elementary students who are experiencing learning difficulties or who are immature is to have them repeat a grade—a policy known as retention. In California, over 40,000 kindergarten and first grade students were retained in 1988-89, an average of more than one child per class of 30.

Undoubtedly, this policy has been carried out with the best of intentions, but extensive research in its downstream consequences clearly demonstrates that it is educationally counterproductive. Not only do children who are retained show lower self-esteem and poorer attitudes toward school than matched classmates who were promoted but also they do less well academically after the experience, which is the crucial point in discrediting the retention strategy. Retention worsens rather than improves student achievement. These results pertain to both repetition of the same grade and two-year programs in kindergarten and first grade. Retained students who are otherwise matched by background, sex, and achievement level with promoted students are more likely to drop out of school by ninth grade by as much as 30 percent.[8]

In short, retention, even when undertaken very early in the child's education, does not work. It creates the illusion of addressing the problems of low-achieving students but, in reality, merely subjects them to a repeat of the same instructional practices and curriculum that failed them the first time around. The better choice, as already described, is to give students the extra help they may need early so that they can stay with their age-mates and continue benefiting from regular classroom instruction. California's elementary schools spend in the vicinity of a quarter of a billion dollars each year to underwrite the added cost of educating retained students. This money should be used where it could do the most good—in delivering the thinking curriculum to underachieving students urgently in need of its stimulating appeal.

An alternative to retention is an idea that began with the little red schoolhouse and enjoyed a following in the 1960s: mixed-aged classrooms in the primary years. This approach is making a comeback in the 1990s. Kentucky and Tennessee have each announced plans to install a system of

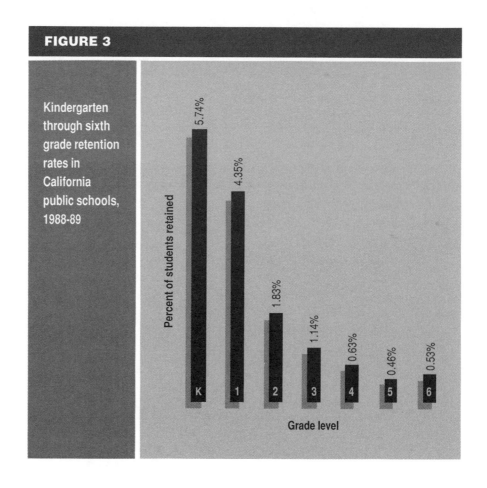

FIGURE 3

Kindergarten through sixth grade retention rates in California public schools, 1988-89

Percent of students retained

5.74%
4.35%
1.83%
1.14%
0.63%
0.46%
0.53%

K   1   2   3   4   5   6

Grade level

ungraded primary schools in the near future. Several strong theoretical justifications support this movement:

- Mixed-age classes make sense from the point of view of cognitive development. Children in the early years of school do not learn at the same rate. In fact, their mental ages may vary as much as four years from their chronological ones. Granted this range, it makes little sense to place children in fixed grade levels at an early age, especially if the result is retention and an early sense of failure. It is better to extend the age range of a primary class and thereby provide a nurturing, success-oriented environment for children at widely diverging developmental levels.
- Nongraded classrooms offer a better social setting, advocates say. Because older children help younger ones, who in turn emulate the older ones, a multiage setting encourages the development of pro-social attitudes of responsibility and tolerance. Research shows that children spontaneously tend to choose the more familial mixed-age social setting over same-age ones. Furthermore, in classes where one teacher stays with the same students for several years, the relationship often becomes so personal that both academic and disciplinary problems lessen.
- It is virtually impossible to teach a mixed-age class using a teacher-centered, lecture-and-workbook approach. For that reason, mixed-age groupings force the issue of improving instructional practice—by means of frequent regroupings of students for active learning tasks, cooperative learning activities, peer and cross-age tutoring, individualized attention, and other instructional strategies alluded to in this chapter of *It's Elementary!*

Not only do children who are retained show lower self-esteem and poorer attitudes toward school than matched classmates who were promoted but also they do less well academically after the experience, which is the crucial point in discrediting the retention strategy.

For Further Information

Cushman, Kathleen. "The Whys and Hows of the Multi-Age Primary Classroom," *American Educator*, Vol. 14 (Summer, 1990), 28–32.

Flunking Grades: Research and Policies on Retention. Edited by L. A. Shepard and M. L. Smith. Philadelphia: The Falmer Press, 1989.

Holmes, C.Thomas, and Kenneth M. Matthews. "The Effects of Nonpromotion on Elementary and Junior High School Pupils: A Meta-Analysis," *Review of Educational Research,* Vol. 54 (Summer, 1984), 225–236.

Program Advisory —Retention of Students in Elementary and Middle Grades. Sacramento: California Department of Education, September 16, 1991.

Shepard, Lorrie, and Mary Lee Smith. "Synthesis of Research on Grade Retention," *Educational Leadership,* Vol. 46 (May, 1990), 84–88.

Smith, Mary Lee, and Lorrie A. Shepard. "What Doesn't Work: Explaining Policies of Retention in the Early Grades," *Phi Delta Kappan*, (October, 1987), 129–134.

Technology and the Thinking Curriculum

The modern tools of the teaching trade go well beyond chalkboard and chalk. These days they include desktop computers, videocassette recorders, handy-cams, laser disk players, overhead projectors with liquid crystal displays, and large screen monitors. School districts that support the purchase of the equipment and teachers who put high-tech devices to work deepening their students' conceptual understandings will find it easier to reach their ambitious educational goals.

RECOMMENDATION

15 **Invest shrewdly in technology to help promote the thinking curriculum.**

Electronic knowledge processing and retrieval systems with accompanying educational software can amplify the elementary school teacher's instructional capabilities in many ways. The computer serves as a valuable classroom management aid in handling such chores as attendance and recordkeeping. In some districts, teachers are using the computer's networking capability to set up electronic bulletin boards that serve them as a resource bank and tool for curricular planning. The computer can also help in sensitive diagnostic applications. For instance, computers can save early drafts of writing assignments as students work toward a finished product. The record thus created can be used to analyze valuable false starts and map out a suitable course for future learnings.

For children, technological tools provide several means for California's elementary schools to support the thinking curriculum. For example, students:

- Use document processors to prepare, revise, and communicate the written word.
- Simulate lab experiments in ideal conditions without the danger of blowing themselves up; e.g., a perfect vacuum or a frictionless world where the laws of Newtonian physics become more apparent.
- Role-play as world leaders in historic times or make city planning decisions for a major metropolitan area and then observe the consequences.
- Videotape a school performance, dub in titles and credits, and then make the final product available for community viewing at the local video store.
- Use nutrient analysis software to analyze their own meals and diets.

- Use laser disks, large screen monitors, and VCRs to retrieve and manipulate visual images of historic events or natural phenomena.
- Gain access to areas of the curriculum in which their teachers may not be well-versed—e.g., a foreign language—by means of a wide variety of instructional video programs.

As the examples above from California schools suggest, the use of technology in the elementary classroom has made great strides in the last decade. To continue progress on this front, however, the schools need to

The Sky's the Limit

Skyline Elementary School, south of San Francisco, is a model technology school for science, kindergarten through grades six. How does elementary grades science instruction look in this setting? On any given day you might find:

- In kindergarten, students plant acorns as part of a schoolwide environmental education unit. Older students from the video club film the event as they did the earlier gathering of the acorns. The resulting film will record the early stages in the life cycle of a tree.

- In first grade, students do a hands-on experiment with magnets as the teacher shows slides from a videodisc to review main concepts.

- In second grade, students use a word processing program to write sentences using their new space vocabulary. The creations are read out loud and then printed out together to make a class booklet.

- In third grade, students take turns clapping hands and then whistling in front of a sound probe. They compare the different shapes the sound waves make on the computer screen.

- In fourth grade, students are building a model of a windshield wiper using Legos. They then attempt to program the computer to run the model with two wipers.

- In fifth grade, students use the endangered species data base to figure out a successful survival plan for bighorn sheep. They study a map and compare it with the animals' requirements to reach their conclusion, which is displayed on a graph.

- In sixth grade, students use a Hypercard stack to search a videodisc for pictures of erupting volcanoes. They will transfer these to a videotape report that their group is preparing about Mt. Shasta. The final product will become part of the school's library of instructional tapes.

Adapted from "Technology Optimizes Performance in Science" by Conrad Mezzetta. Reprinted with permission from the fall, 1989 issue of *California Technology Project Quarterly*, pp. 32–33.

overcome three important obstacles. First, educational software programs need to be improved. Too often, they have been focused on low-level skills applications rather than inquiry-based ones that promote student engagement with new ideas. Second, teachers need better access to technology. Only half the nation's teachers report ever having used a computer. Only one-third have had as little as ten hours training in computer applications. Where technological aids have been made available, however, teachers have been quick to make use of them. Third, the elementary schools need to acquire more equipment. Ironically, the state that has been a cradle of high-tech innovation in the post-war era ranks among the bottom quarter in its student-to-computer ratio—currently estimated at about 23 to 1. Some experts suggest that the best ratio is two or three students for every one work station.[9]

Technology is a tool for improving curriculum and instruction, not an end in itself. Teachers should be careful as they select technology-based

The Freedom Machine

For certain special education students, computers serve as "freedom machines" because they help make communication itself possible. Before being provided access to a word processor, Jami, a student with a disability, spent hours writing his spelling words because he was unable to grip a pencil (see writing sample).

Through the Daedalus Project Jami was provided with a computer, instruction on keyboarding, word processing, and writing skills following the Daedalus Writing Curriculum. What follows is an article Jami wrote for the *Daedalus Newsletter* during a retreat in March, 1987.

materials to ensure that the materials remain consistent with the precepts of the thinking curriculum. A software program which emphasizes multiple-choice or fill-in-the-blank responses is no better on a computer screen than on a ditto sheet. Fortunately, improved software is becoming available. As the Task Force looks to the future, it foresees an increasingly prominent role for technology in increasing the productivity of teachers and expanding the student's learning world.

For Further Information

Bruder, Isabelle. "Guide to Multimedia: How It's Changing the Way We Teach and Learn," *Electronic Learning,* Vol. 11 (September, 1991), 22.

California Model Academic Technology Programs. Sacramento: California Department of Education, 1991. Video, 6 minutes.

Computer Applications Planning. Adapted by the Educational Technology Unit, California Department of Education, from a document published by the

WRESTLEMANIA III, March 29, 1987

BE THERE!!!!!

On March 29, 1987, in the Pontiac Silver dome in Michigan, there will be 90,000 screaming fans suffering from Hulkamania!!!! The feature match will be between Hulk Hogan and the 8th Wonder of the World: Andre the Giant. Andre the Giant is undefeated in his professional career which has lasted 15 years. Hulk Hogan, on the other hand, has been the champion of the WWF for the past three years. It should be a darn good match between the 7'4", 507 pound giant, and the 6'8", 325 pound Hulkster. You can be sure that Hulkamania will be running wild!!!!!!!

"Jami is our first published author," his teacher proudly noted a few weeks later. "He has an article and a poem coming out in an upcoming JAYCEEs magazine."

Based on text excerpted from ConnSense Bulletin: Connecticut's *Special Education Network for Software Evaluation*, Vol. 5, No. 1 (October, 1987), Storrs, Conn.: University of Connecticut. The excerpt appeared in *Power On! New Tools for Teaching and Learning*, a summary of a report to the Hundredth Congress (September, 1988), p. 13.

Merrimack Education Center. Sacramento: California Department of Education, 1985.

Educator's Guide for Evaluating Educational Technology Programs (Guide and video). California Technology Project Assessment Team. Chico: California State University, Chico, 1990.

Power On! New Tools for Teaching and Learning. Summary of a report to the Hundredth Congress of the United States, Office of Technology Assessment, (September, 1988).

Reading, Literature, and Television: A Powerful Partnership. Los Angeles: RETAC, Los Angeles County Office of Education, 1990.

Strategic Plan for Information Technology. Sacramento: California Department of Education, 1991.

A Window on the Future of Education. Sacramento: California Department of Education, 1991. Video, 13 minutes (The California Model Technology Schools Project).

ALL IN THE PROFESSION

CHANGING THE CURRICULUM IS EASY TO DO—ON PAPER. THE MOST
important thing that counts in improving elementary education,
however, is what happens once the classroom door closes and the
school day begins. A fundamental goal of the thinking curriculum is
to make school a child-centered place where the student is consistently encouraged to play an active role in his or her own learning. In
order to accomplish this end, however, the reform strategies themselves must be *teacher*-centered. This reflects the reality that the
elementary teacher, more than anyone else, decides what takes place
in the classroom.

The purpose of this chapter is to focus on the pivotal issue of
supporting the growth of teaching as a profession in California as the
most direct route to improving the state's elementary schools. The
Elementary Grades Task Force's discussion and recommendations in
this area fall into two main categories: how best to support change
among the present cadre of elementary teachers and how to improve
the recruitment and induction of new teachers into the profession.

A Look at the Status Quo

The situation of public school teachers in California has been the focus of several reports in recent years, most notably in the California Commission on the Teaching Profession's report, *Who Will Teach Our Children?* Although it is not the intent to review the Commission's report in detail here, it is important to note the most significant findings.

On the bright side, elementary teachers are better compensated in California than was the case a decade ago. Teachers' salaries in the state currently rank among the highest in the nation. New opportunities for growth within the profession have been opened up by such innovations as the Mentor Teacher Program and Subject Matter Projects. An increasing number of top college candidates are training to become teachers.

On the other hand, many nagging factors continue to undermine the average teacher's sense of professionalism:

1. *Isolation*. As a rule, elementary teachers feel isolated in their classrooms. For many, the only regular chance to exchange ideas with other adults comes during their daily half-hour lunch break. In a survey conducted by the California Commission on the Teaching Profession, 80 percent of the teachers endorsed the concept of visiting, or being observed by, fellow teachers as a good way to sharpen their classroom techniques; but only 20 percent reported having had the opportunity to do so.
2. *Class size*. Teachers may feel isolated in the classroom but they are certainly not alone. With an average of 28.3 students in each elementary classroom, California's public school system ranks 49th

Teacher Professionalism?

It is amazing that in 1991, with the technology available to us, most teachers have to wait in line in the school office to make a phone call to a parent. What other professional is left without a phone in his or her work station? At a time when personal computers are essential to almost every knowledgeable worker, teachers don't even have phones! Instead, many spend their own money on teaching supplies because they lack control over the budget. The recent Carnegie Foundation study (1990) found more than 70 percent of all teachers in the U.S. are not involved deeply in decisions about curriculum, staff development, grouping of students, promotion and retention policies, or school budgets.

Quoted from "Pretending Not to Know What We Know," by Carl Glickman. Reprinted with approval from the May, 1991 issue of *Educational Leadership*, p. 7. Copyright by Association for Supervision and Curriculum Development.

out of 50 states in terms of class size. This number has increased by almost two full students since 1987-88. Larger classes make it more difficult for teachers to provide the individual attention to learning needs that students want and deserve.[1]

3. *Lack of instructional materials.* The shortage of instructional materials, ranging from textbooks, video equipment, and maps and globes to (by the end of the school year) such basics as paper and chalk, is endemic. Although data on the extent to which teachers spend their own money on materials are hard to find, the current average may be close to that of a New Orleans teacher who laments, "By a conservative estimate, I spend $800 of my salary on materials."[2]

4. *No career ladder.* The lack of opportunities for advancement within the profession is a continuing concern for many teachers. Although the Mentor Teacher Program—with over 10,000 teachers participating statewide—has helped matters immensely, many teachers still find that the only way to continue earning salary increases is to abandon their first love in education and go into administration.

5. *Lack of autonomy.* Finally, and most pervasively of all, many teachers feel cut off from a sense of professionalism by their perceived lack of autonomy. In too many school districts, teachers are treated as technicians or assembly-line workers. They are supplied with materials, assigned tightly defined learning tasks, and monitored for their ability to produce favorable test results for the various "customers" of the administration: the school board, taxpayers, and parents. Decisions that directly affect what takes place in the classroom—which topics will be taught, which text-books will be used, how classes will be scheduled, and how a teacher's performance will be measured—are made elsewhere.

The lack of opportunities for advancement within the profession is a continuing concern for many teachers.

For Further Information

"The Future of the Teaching Profession," *Educational Leadership*, Vol. 46 (November, 1988), entire issue.

A Nation Prepared: Teachers for the 21st Century, the Report of the Task Force on Teaching as a Profession. New York: Carnegie Forum on Education and the Economy, 1986.

Racial or Ethnic Distribution of Staff and Students in California Public Schools 1990-91. Compiled from the California Basic Educational Data System. Sacramento: California Department of Education, 1991.

Who Will Teach Our Children? A Strategy for Improving California's Schools: The Report of the California Commission on the Teaching Profession. Dorman L. Commons, Chair of the Commission. Sacramento: California Commission on the Teaching Profession, 1985.

Supporting Professional Growth

There are over 130,000 elementary teachers in California's public schools. The majority will remain in the classroom until they retire. Clearly, if a meaning-centered curriculum is to become a reality in the classroom over the next decade (instead of just another educational reform pipe dream), then elementary teachers now in the system must become that curriculum's foremost advocates and practitioners.

RECOMMENDATION

16 **Provide teachers access to the best thinking about curriculum and instructional practices.**

A *thinking curriculum* is not an off-the-shelf textbook-driven affair. Teaching to stimulate children's interest rather than assigning chapters to be read and doling out workbook exercises to be completed eats up a teacher's inventory of new ideas and resources at a voracious clip. Teachers who have attempted to present the thinking curriculum report feeling the need for more preparation time, more help from their peers, and more subject-matter knowledge.

Traditionally, new ideas about excellent curricular and instructional practice, when they reached elementary teachers at all, did so by means of staff development programs. In the past, these programs often consisted of after-school or weekend presentations put together by non-teacher "experts" on topics that were often unrelated to the pressing instructional issues at the school. Typically, little opportunity existed for the teacher-audience to practice what the lecturers told them and no provision for follow-up over an extended period.

Fortunately, in California the futility of one-shot staff development programs was recognized in the 1980s, and an effort was mounted to devise a more effective professional development alternative. In recent years, an infrastructure of subject-matter projects has been developed that, to date, include the California Arts, Foreign Language, History–Social Science, Literature, Mathematics, Science, and Writing projects. In each of these subject areas, teachers can attend intensive, three-to-four week institutes that focus on the latest ideas in the discipline and their classroom applications. The experiences at these institutes are then supported by one or two years of follow-up meetings in which teachers have the opportunity to try out the new approaches in the crucible of their own classrooms; to be observed and talk over results with peers; to report to the group; to modify

Clearly, if a meaning-centered curriculum is to become a reality in the classroom over the next decade, then elementary teachers now in the system must become that curriculum's foremost advocates and practitioners.

their thinking; and, in general, to consolidate their insights to reach a new professional equilibrium. The Subject Matter Projects provide a forum that teachers use to exchange ideas and craft insights about what constitutes the best instructional practice in a given area of the curriculum.

While access to each of the Subject-Matter Projects is limited to only a few hundred teachers every year, the indirect leavening effect of the programs is undoubtedly much greater. When "graduates" return to their schools, they become resources for their fellow faculty members to draw on. This exchange can happen formally—by designating lead teachers by grade level—and works best when two people from a school go through an institute together. The point is, few elementary teachers will ever have time to develop a state-of-the-art expertise in all curricular and instructional areas of interest, but as individual teachers become specialists in a disci-

Sharing the Craft Knowledge

A main reason Asian lessons are so well crafted is that there is a very systematic effort to pass on the accumulated wisdom of teaching practice to each new generation of teachers by providing teachers the opportunities to continually learn from each other. One mechanism is through meetings organized by head teachers at their own schools. A glimpse at what takes place in these study groups was provided in a conversation we recently had with a Japanese teacher. She and her colleagues spend a good deal of their time together working on lesson plans. After they finish a plan, one teacher from the group teaches the lesson to her students while the others look on. Afterward, the group meets again to criticize the teacher's performance and make suggestions for how the lesson could be improved. In her school, there is an annual "teaching fair." Teachers from other schools are invited to visit the school and observe the lessons being taught. The visitors rate the lessons and the teacher with the best lesson is declared the winner. In addition, national television in Japan presents programs that show how master teachers handle particular lessons or concepts.

Making use of lessons that have been honed over time does not mean that the Asian teacher simply mimics what he or she sees. As with great actors or musicians, the substance of the curriculum becomes the script or the score; the goal is to perform the role or piece as effectively and creatively as possible.

Adapted from "How Asian Teachers Polish Each Lesson to Perfection" by James W. Stigler and Harold W. Stevenson. Reprinted with permission from the spring, 1991 issue of the *American Educator*, the quarterly journal of the American Federation of Teachers, p. 46.

Subject Matter Projects

California Arts Project

Marin County Office of Education
1111 Las Gallinas Avenue
San Rafael, CA 94913
(415) 499-5893

California Foreign Language Project

Stanford University
Littlefield Center, Room 14
300 Lasuen Street
Stanford, CA 94305-5013
(415) 723-4581

California History–Social Science Project

University of California
Gayley Center, Suite 304
405 Hilgard Avenue
Los Angeles, CA 90024-1372
(213) 206-5031

California Literature Project

University of California, San Diego
9500 Gilman Drive
La Jolla, CA 92093-1415
(619) 534-1660

California Mathematics Project

University of California
Office of the President
300 Lakeside Drive, 18th Floor
Oakland, CA 94612-3550
(510) 987-9350

California Science Project

University of California
Office of the President
300 Lakeside Drive, 18th Floor
Oakland, CA 94612-3550
(510) 987-9510

California Writing Project

University of California
School of Education
Berkeley, CA 94720
(510) 642-0963

pline over the years and share that knowledge with their colleagues, the entire teaching and learning enterprise at a school is enriched. Teacher specialization at the elementary level, when supported by such high quality professional development as the Subject Matter Projects, is proving to be an effective way to improve curriculum and instruction.

Finally, it should be remembered that some of the most effective professional development activities involve just plain reading—keeping abreast of the top journals, newsletters, and selected literature in the educational field. Schools and districts can encourage this practice through the cost-effective strategy of keeping teachers' libraries well stocked with

The Teaching Profession circa 1998: A Scenario

Mary Jones teaches in the ungraded primary at Shepherd Elementary School in a medium-sized urban district. There are three teams of two teachers each in the primary group. Each team is responsible for 50 youngsters over the three-year period that they are in the primary group. Ms. Jones's day is divided among classroom teaching responsibilities, individual tutorials with students in her team, and professional development time spent in a variety of different ways.

Each week, Ms. Jones spends approximately 25 percent of her time working with fellow teachers. Today she is "presenting" at the Wednesday morning diagnostics group meeting. She has carefully assembled a portfolio appraising Jimmy's ability to deal with specific number concepts. She even has some videotape of Jimmy working in a small group to illustrate her points. The other teachers in the group have a chance to ask questions and make suggestions.

In this case, one of the teachers remembers reading a recent article in *Education Researcher* dealing with similar problems, but she cannot remember the exact reference. The teachers are meeting in the Teacher Resource Room; one pulls up the education data base on the computer, identifies the article, and a hard copy is printed in a matter of minutes.

The meeting's second presentation deals with difficulties organizing cooperative small groups. The 40-minute meeting closes with a reminder that applications for the school-based teacher development grants are due next Friday. With these grants, teachers interested in doing observations in other schools may apply for funds to cover travel costs and the cost of substitute teachers.

When she returns to her classroom, Ms. Jones finds that five 11-year olds have arrived to work with the small science groups. Cross-age tutoring has become a regular part of the instructional program at topical research papers. Teachers can promote the process themselves by forming professional study groups to discuss books of mutual interest and share insights about the current literature.

For Further Information

Joyce, Bruce, and others. "Synthesis of Research on Staff Development: A Framework for Future Study and State-Of-The-Art Analysis," *Educational Leadership*, Vol. 45 (November, 1987), 77–87.

Little, Judith W., and others. *Staff Development in California, Policy Analysis for California Education (PACE), Executive Summary.* San Francisco: Far West Laboratory for Educational Research and Development, 1987.

Shepherd Elementary. In addition to student benefits, the program has become a vehicle of communication between primary and intermediate teachers as they discuss how different participants are doing.

After the children have gone home for the day, Ms. Jones gets ready for tomorrow's meeting of the school-based management team on which she serves this year. Over coffee in the lounge, she informally discusses with colleagues the pros and cons of the meeting's agenda: a proposal for more frequent assessments to catch students who are slipping behind in reading in the primary grades.

Returning to her desk in the office she shares with two colleagues, Ms. Jones answers some phone calls. Two are from parents concerning their children's work and one is from John Clark, a middle school teacher. Clark has called about arranging the next meeting of the professional study group to which he and Ms. Jones belong. The purpose of the group—modeled on those common in the law, medicine, and social work fields—is to keep current on professional literature and books that are of mutual interest to the members.

That night at home, Ms. Jones picks up the mail and turns immediately to the letters exchange page of the bimonthly journal on teaching. She looks for her letter responding to another reader's inquiry regarding the benefits of teaching the same primary age children for two or three years. These letters are really mini-articles, and the exchanges go on for months. Some of the responses have provided excellent suggestions and insights for Ms. Jones in her practice. She is pleased to see her letter is there.

Adapted from "Staff Development and the Restructured School," by Albert Shanker, president of the American Federation of Teachers, AFL-CIO. Reprinted with permission from the ASCD 1990 Yearbook, *Changing School Culture Through Staff Development*, pp. 93–96. Copyright by Association for Supervision and Curriculum Development .

It should be remembered that some of the most effective professional development activities involve just plain reading— keeping abreast of the top journals, newsletters, and selected literature in the educational field.

RECOMMENDATION

17 **Make sure that teachers have adequate scheduled time for working together in professional collaborations at the school site.**

The changes implied by the thinking curriculum ought not and, ultimately, cannot be forced on school personnel. Teachers need and deserve the autonomy to choose and enact changes on the basis of their individual and collective judgment. The most important and enduring kinds of professional development—those that enhance professional judgment and that result in improved student outcomes—must go on for years, not weeks or months, with repeated opportunities for input, discussion, application, and review. All of this implies a fundamental alteration in teachers' working conditions. Specifically, it requires that teachers have more time for professional development, including time for long-range planning, for taking stock, and for additional training.

Where will the time teachers need for professional development come from? The recommendation most often presented to the Task Force—that there should be ten to twenty compensated professional development days in addition to the 180 days of instruction—is a good one and one which the Task Force endorses. But it is quite expensive. The system-wide price tag for each additional day of teachers' time in California is approximately $55 million. In the best of all possible worlds, of course, the importance of educational leaders investing capital in the development of their front-line human talent would be universally recognized, and such substantial sums would be immediately forthcoming. Pending the arrival of that day, however, several interim policy choices are available to schools and school districts to make time for professional development:

1. *Staff development days.* Schools can take better advantage of the eight staff development days available to most of them under AB 777, the School Based Coordination Act. Right now, most elementary schools use only two to four of these days per year—usually in the classic workshop format that finds experts lecturing to faculty members on single-issue topics for a few hours and with no provision for long-term follow-up. A more judicious use of this time would be to provide one complete day a month for teachers (many of whom are already well-versed in the fundamental principles of the thinking curriculum, anyway) to work together with colleagues on practical questions of application. Such a self-designed program would have several advantages. In all likelihood, it would provide greater continuity in the staff development effort over the school year; it would improve the probability that instructional issues of

primary importance at the particular school site would be addressed; and it would put the leadership responsibility for the continuing growth of the school's teaching core where it belongs—on the teacher-professionals themselves.

2. *Creative use of categorical funds.* Schools can reexamine how they spend categorical funds, with an eye toward buying teachers some released time to visit one another's classes or schools. Indeed, the Task Force concurs with Robert Slavin's recommendation that districts and schools should earmark 25 percent of all categorical funds for a variety of professional development activities.[3] For

The California Science Implementation Network

If teaching elementary students that all rocks can be classified as either igneous, metamorphic, or sedimentary isn't good science instruction, what is? California's *Science Framework* offers some answers. As impressive as it is to lift, however, the *Science Framework* will have little real impact on elementary science education here until a critical mass of teachers is persuaded to put its ideas into practice in the classroom. How can this conversion process be accelerated? The California Science Implementation Network (CSIN) is a statewide program for assisting elementary schools deliver a high quality science program that systematically acquaints students with the "big ideas" in the life, earth, and physical sciences. It also may be a good model for how other disciplines can answer the framework implementation challenge.

CSIN is a network. Under its umbrella, schools interested in upgrading their elementary science program have banded together to share implementation ideas and experiences.

CSIN is also a process. Its major premise is that installing a constructivist science framework is a long-term project—to be undertaken over several years with identified benchmarks of progress to keep the effort on track. Teachers in CSIN schools write their own science curricula guided by a program elements and content matrix that, once completed, serves as a road map to the instructional future.

Finally, CSIN is an implementation system. Teachers' preparation for and support during the change process typically consists of a week-long summer session held at a regional location, followed by three meetings during the academic year and on-site visitations from Science Staff Developers, as requested. The CSIN philosophy is that what science educators most need in implementing the new science curriculum is the opportunity to trade notes, exchange information, and learn from one another's experiences. So far, 800 elementary schools have joined the network.

The most important and enduring kinds of professional development—those that enhance professional judgment and that result in improved student outcomes—must go on for years, not weeks or months, with repeated opportunities for input, discussion, application, and review.

example, a school can use some of its categorical funds to hire part-time specialist teachers in such areas as art, music, or physical education. When the specialist takes over a class, the regular teacher is able to visit and observe colleagues. Giving teachers the opportunity to see innovative programs in process is one of the most powerful ways of motivating teachers to take a chance in their own instructional approaches. (Effective staff development does *not* require that every teacher be out of the classroom at the same time.) ECIA Chapter 1 funds can also be used to pay eligible teachers stipends for attending the summer institutes of Subject Matter Projects.

3. *Accumulation of blocks of time.* Schools can accumulate small increments of instructional time daily by extending the school day. The "surplus" time thus created can be expended in bigger blocks for professional development purposes.

4. *Other strategies.* Student-free opportunities can also be created by occasionally doubling up on team-taught classes and by having school administrators or mentor teachers pinch-hit in the classroom.

Providing common planning time to teachers of the same grade level is critical.

Providing common planning time to teachers of the same grade level is critical. Sharing at least one preparation period a week is necessary to allow teachers to engage in on-going conversations about curriculum, the needs of individual students, and the best way to coordinate resources. This is also a time for teachers to share ideas about instructional practices and discuss any difficulties they may be experiencing in their classrooms. To this end, schools should consider using their School Improvement Program or ECIA Chapter 1 funds to provide released time for teachers to engage in curriculum development and grade-level planning. These funds may also be used to provide stipends to teachers to do curriculum development or grade-level planning during the summer, during off-track time for year-round teachers, or at other times.

For Further Information

Changing School Culture Through Staff Development. 1990 Yearbook of the Association for Supervision and Curriculum Development. Alexandria, Va.: Association for Supervision and Curriculum Development, 1990.

Karant, Vicki I. "Supervision in the Age of Teacher Empowerment," *Educational Leadership*, Vol. 46 (May, 1989), 27–29.

Stigler, James W., and Harold W. Stevenson. "How Asian Teachers Polish Each Lesson to Perfection," *American Educator* (spring, 1991), 12–47.

RECOMMENDATION

18 **Support teacher professionalism with a classroom supply budget, secretarial help, and a well-equipped workplace.**

As previously noted, elementary teachers are hindered from carrying out their educational mission by an assortment of obstacles that would be unimaginable for a comparably skilled worker in the business sector. These handicaps to productivity include cramped or nonexistent work space at the school; a lack of access to such basic technological aids as the telephone or copying machines; and a perennial shortage of classroom materials. Clearly, it is penny-wise and pound-foolish to hire a professionally trained and remunerated teacher and then burn up his or her time by having the person monitor the cafeteria or perform perfunctory clerical tasks. At a minimum, teachers should be supported at the school site in a manner befitting their professional status by providing them with a quiet office space; a comfortable faculty commons area in which to exchange ideas with peers; access to a telephone, word-processor or computer, copying machines, and other technology; and "on call" secretarial help. Teachers should also have at their disposal a discretionary budget for purchasing classroom supplies and supplementary instructional materials.

The path to increasing the professional skills of today's elementary school teachers is not an easy one, but it is clearly marked: provide teachers access to ideas and time to work with those ideas in a supportive environment. But what about the future? What about new teachers joining the profession?

SECTION TWO

Recruiting and Retaining Teachers

Student enrollments are soaring. Assuming that California's already high pupil-teacher ratio remains constant (instead of being lowered, as would be advisable), districts in the state will need to hire 37,500 new elementary teachers in the first half of the 1990s.

RECOMMENDATION

19 **Aggressively recruit teachers from a diversity of ethnic backgrounds.**

Meeting the demand for new teachers with talented, committed, and knowledgeable recruits poses a number of challenges. Among the most significant of these is establishing an educational work force that more accurately reflects the ethnic make-up of the student population. Right now, a serious mismatch exists. Whites constitute about half the student population but 82 percent of the teachers. Hispanics, on the other hand, make up more than 30 percent of the student population but just over 7 percent of the teachers. Indeed, *all* minorities are underrepresented in the public school teaching ranks in terms of their relative share of the student population. Among other things, a direct consequence of this recruiting failure is a critical shortage in the number of teachers with the bilingual skills to instruct limited-English-proficient students. The recruitment of new teachers, particularly from minority groups, must become a top priority in California.[4]

Several initiatives to begin achieving greater parity in schools' faculties have been undertaken. They include strategies to identify minority students who are potential teachers in the middle grades and high schools and encourage them to consider teaching as a career. For instance, the Pool of Recruitable Teachers (PORT) Program, supported by a Carnegie grant to California State University, Dominguez Hills, works with middle schools to improve academic achievement of minority students. Promising middle school students then gain a sense of what teaching is like by tutoring elementary school students in the district. Similar programs—often involving partnerships among the public schools, the California Community Colleges, the California State University, the University of California, and business sponsors—are springing up around the state. Project Socrates in Los Angeles or the Minority Teacher Recruiting Program in the Bay Area are examples. Districts have also offered incentives for instructional aides to complete their college credits and become teachers—an especially valuable approach to recruiting bilingual teachers.

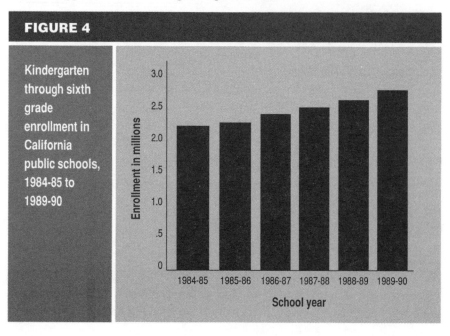

FIGURE 4

Kindergarten through sixth grade enrollment in California public schools, 1984-85 to 1989-90

FIGURE 5

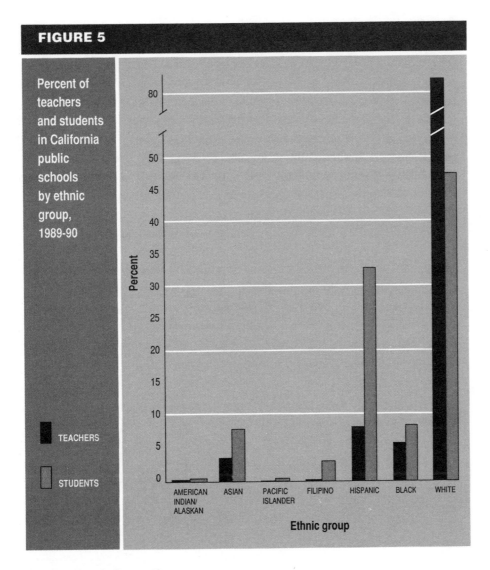

Percent of teachers and students in California public schools by ethnic group, 1989-90

Percent

■ TEACHERS

☐ STUDENTS

80
50
45
40
35
30
25
20
15
10
5
0

AMERICAN INDIAN/ ALASKAN   ASIAN   PACIFIC ISLANDER   FILIPINO   HISPANIC   BLACK   WHITE

Ethnic group

For Further Information

Remedying the Shortage of Teachers for Limited-English-Proficient Students.
    Sacramento: California Department of Education, 1991.
Toward a More Diverse Faculty for California's Schools, Colleges, and Universities:
    Programs to Prepare Underrepresented Students for Careers in Teaching.
    Prepared by Intersegmental Coordinating Council. Sacramento: California
    Department of Education, 1991.

RECOMMENDATION

20 **Support new teachers.**

    Traditionally, new teachers are given the teaching assignments no
one else wants, a set of classroom keys, and a wide berth. "Young teachers
are often forced to search on their own for survival tactics once they are on

the job," the report of the California Commission on the Teaching Profession noted in 1985.[5] While this situation still prevails in many cases, a pilot program to help beginning teachers during the first critical year of on-the-job experience—when, typically, the highest attrition in their numbers takes place—is showing remarkable results. The California New Teacher Project (CNTP), which includes 37 different pilot programs around the state affecting 1,900 new teachers thus far, is replacing the old "sink or swim" mentality of teacher induction with a broadly supportive one.

In a prototype example of the CNTP, new teachers receive assistance from mentors throughout the year, released time to observe experienced teachers, continuing education seminars to troubleshoot recurring problems, and a supplemental stipend for the purchase of instructional materials. The results have been gratifying. New teachers in the various pilot projects have shown a 95 percent return rate to teaching in their second year—compared with a 70 percent return rate for new teachers statewide.

The new teacher program is one element in a lifelong career ladder envisioned in the report of the California Commission on the Teaching Profession, *Who Will Teach Our Children?* Rungs on such a ladder might lead from a teaching residency of a couple of years duration to the following:

- Earning of tenure
- Earning of "board certified" status in one's specialty from the National Board of Professional Teaching Standards
- Assuming responsibility in curriculum development, school governance, staff development, or peer evaluation
- Taking a sabbatical year of work-study in a field related to one's academic interest
- Being recognized as a "lead" teacher or mentor

Obviously, we are a long way from the full realization of such a vision. But the direction the schools should be heading is clear—and implies a willingness and capacity among teachers to grow within their profession over a lifetime.

For Further Information

Designing Programs for New Teachers: The California Experience. Edited by Ann Morey and Diane Murphy. San Francisco: Far West Laboratory for Educational Research and Policy Development, 1990.

New Teacher Success: You Can Make a Difference. Edited by Sue Garmston and Carol Bartell. Sacramento: California Department of Education, Commission on Teacher Credentialing, and the California New Teacher Project, 1991.

Passage into Teaching (videotape). Sacramento: California Department of Education and Commission on Teacher Credentialing, 1990.

MEASURES FOR SUCCESS

A BASIC RULE OF EDUCATION IS THAT "WHAT YOU TEST IS WHAT YOU GET."
The explanation for this phenomenon is rooted in human nature.
When teachers and administrators know their professional compe-
tence is going to be judged on the basis of how well their students
perform on a given test, they naturally tend to concentrate on priming
their students to excel on that type of test—whatever lofty sentiments
the curriculum frameworks or the school's mission statement may
espouse. The problem with many assessment instruments used at the
elementary school level is that they still reinforce the old skills-based
curriculum. Multiple-choice tests that require students to fill in
bubbles on machine-graded answer sheets have tended to put a
premium on rudimentary academic skills—the ability to spell correctly, to recall the multiplication tables, to distinguish between an
adjective and an adverb, to name the presidents. At the same time,
teachers have not been spurred by such tests to foster their students'
capacities to perform the generative acts of analysis, organization,
communication, creativity, and other higher order thinking processes
that are the hallmark of a rich, meaning-centered curriculum.

Clearly, managing the transition to a thinking curriculum will
entail creating a new assessment system as well. The purpose of this
chapter is to describe important progress being made in this area and
to provide a vision of exemplary assessment practice at the elementary level in the 1990s.

A Progress Report

California is in the midst of making a fundamental revision of its assessment program at the elementary school level. The purpose of these changes is to develop an assessment scheme consistent with the ambitious goals of the thinking curriculum. What will such an "authentic" assessment program look like? To be sure, a definitive answer to this question can be obtained only through experience and through the process of innovation, trial, and refinement now under way in California. In the meantime, however, four principles underlying such a system of monitoring student achievement have already begun to emerge:

1. Assessments in the new system will rely largely on *exemplary tasks* that give information about student performance. For example, in assessing students' understanding of the meaning and historical context of the Gettysburg Address, students might be asked to prepare a television news broadcast of how the event might have been reported using modern technology rather than to simply memorize the speech itself.

2. The tasks assigned will be *complex* (involving the marshaling of many learning behaviors), *open-ended* (with many possible solutions), and intellectually *coherent* (resulting in a single work-product.) These qualities contrast starkly with most norm-referenced exams that ask a battery of unrelated questions, each of which is meant to elicit, in theory at least, a single right answer.

3. The primary functions of assessment are to inform students of their progress in reaching desired performance levels and to help teachers identify what students know and still need to learn. Accordingly, the results of new assessment practices will be *formative*; that is, they will provide a basis for making decisions about the students' future learning needs and not be used, as is too often the case with standardized test results, to sort and select students for segregated learning tracks.

4. Another main function of testing is to provide information to the various clients served by public education, including parents, taxpayers, school board members, and legislators. The results obtained from assessment practices must provide a valid basis for comparisons across classes and schools but not by embracing the false objectivity of fixating on relatively unimportant academic subskills. Accordingly, assessment of the complex repertoire of learning behaviors called for by the thinking curriculum will be

> The primary functions of assessment are to inform students of their progress in reaching desired performance levels and to help teachers identify what students know and still need to learn.

evaluated on the basis of agreed-on criteria while also relying on the *informed professional judgment* of teachers.

Authentic assessment practices of the kind described above are likely to differ from past ones at the elementary level in some surprising ways. They are likely to include integrated reading-writing assessments; the evaluation of student writings or of other work samples collected in portfolios; investigations conducted by small groups of students; and the staging of hands-on problem-solving activities. They are likely to require both on-demand performance from students as well as performances completed over extended periods of time. Questions on authentic tests will not be jealously guarded secrets; they may be known well ahead of time. Speed of response will seldom be at a premium in the assessment instruments of the 1990s; students may demonstrate their scholastic achievement in certain facets of their learning over an entire term. And often, students who consult one another over their answers won't be "cheating"; they will be collaborating in much the same way that professionals in the world of business are expected to do.

The California Department of Education and many teachers, schools, and school districts have been exploring these new forms of assessment

Questions on authentic tests will not be jealously guarded secrets.

Portfolios of Student Work

A portfolio is a collection of representative work. As the word's roots suggest (and as is still the case in the arts), the collection is carried to a place for inspection or exhibit, usually as a kind of resume. In the academic subject areas such as English-language arts or mathematics, a portfolio often serves two distinct purposes: providing a documentation of the student's work, and serving as the basis for evaluation of work-in-progress or work-over-time. The former process commits the student and the teacher to ensure that there is a quasi-public record of the student's work in all the major areas/techniques/genres of the course. The latter purpose takes the next step and suggests what portfolios can do that traditional assessment cannot do: provide direct evidence for evaluating the student's ability to make progress and master essential techniques. It is common in evaluating portfolios that teachers work together to ensure greater reliability in scoring. A procedure used extensively in New Zealand and Australia, where portfolio assessment is common, is to have regional meetings where people bring samples of the best, middle-level, and worst student work at which time grades are re-calibrated, based on a consensus about standards.

Quoted from "On Portfolios," a paper written by Grant Wiggins, director of Programs and Research, Center on Learning, Assessment, and School Structure (CLASS) and published by CLASS, Geneseo, N.Y. Reprinted with permission of the author.

over the last several years. A rich variety of possibilities for performance-based testing and evaluation of student progress are emerging in the major content areas, as described in the paragraphs that follow.

English-language arts. Building on the success of California's Writing Assessment Program, teams of teachers have begun developing new integrated English-language arts assessment tasks for elementary school students. In one of the formats, elementary students are involved in sessions held on three consecutive days in which they participate in group discussions. In response to a wide variety of texts, students read, discuss, write, edit, and rewrite. The California Learning Record, an American version of the British Primary Language Record, helps teachers document student progress as they work on these real world tasks in the classroom.

Science. In the spring of 1990, over 50,000 California sixth graders had the opportunity to demonstrate their understanding of important science concepts by visiting five lab "stations" and performing various hands-on tasks. A similar number of fifth-grade students participated in the spring, 1991 field testing. Teachers who took part in the scoring remarked that it gave them the opportunity to see how well students in other schools and districts fared in handling the identical science challenge and, thus, gave them a better understanding of how well prepared their own students were.

History–social science. During the 1990-91 school year, California elementary school students studying the Revolutionary War participated in pilot testing a series of "jig-saw" performance tasks that asked each group to acquire information, discuss findings, complete in-depth research, and

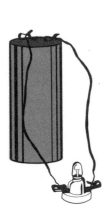

A student at Garden Grove School District, who had just completed the CAP sixth grade performance-based test in science, gave this reaction: "In the hands-on test you could experiment with things rather than just reading a question and picturing something."

Hands-on Science Assessment

What does authentic assessment look like in science? For 50,000 California sixth graders in the spring of 1990, it meant visiting five "stations" to see whether they could perform the following tasks:

1. Build a circuit out of the materials provided; predict which materials conduct electricity; test that hypothesis and record the results.
2. Create a classification system for a collection of leaves and explain the adjustments necessary when a new "mystery" leaf is introduced into the group.
3. Perform tests on a collection of rocks; record the test results, and classify them, based on the information provided.
4. Use a variety of provided equipment to estimate and measure several characteristics of water.
5. Perform a chemical test on samples of lake water to discover why fish are dying.[1]

then prepare a newspaper as if it were from the period. One participating teacher reported, "No one thought the activity was a test! Everyone worked without stopping until the whole class was done."

Mathematics. In the California Assessment Program's (CAP's) current pilot testing, elementary school mathematicians are having their work assessed while completing a variety of investigations. In one pilot test, teams of students are given an open-ended mathematical problem for which they must devise a solution. (See shaded box, "Red Light, Green Light.") Each team works on its solution for about 45 minutes and then prepares an oral presentation of the solution for the whole class. Periodically, as the teams work, the teacher asks questions to gauge on-going understanding. After all teams have reported, the teacher leads a discussion that helps students reevaluate their thinking. The next day, each team writes up its final solution, which is then available for scoring. Another promising strategy being pursued by the California Mathematics Project and CAP is the holistic scoring of student mathematics portfolios.

Physical education. One area where performance assessment has been the norm is physical fitness. Since 1989 almost all California fifth graders have participated in the *California Physical and Health-Related Fitness Test*. The assessment, which consists of five items, is designed to evaluate strength, flexibility, endurance, body composition, and the cardio-respiratory system. The results of this look at the physical fitness of California students has encouraged many elementary schools to give renewed emphasis to their physical education programs.

Visual and performing arts. Portfolio assessment for visual and performing arts began as a result of two symposia on arts assessment sponsored by professional organizations during 1990-91. In selected projects, students and teachers collaboratively identify pieces of creative work that show progress or growth over time. Students answer questions about their selections in journals or sketchbooks: What was I trying to do?

> Another promising strategy being pursued by the California Mathematics Project and CAP is the holistic scoring of student mathematics portfolios.

Red Light, Green Light

This question is an example of an open-ended mathematics problem from the California Assessment Program:

The cycle for the traffic light on Main Street is green for 55 seconds, yellow for 5 seconds, and red for 30 seconds. What is the probability of having to stop at the traffic light? Explain your reasoning and include consideration of how drivers react to yellow lights.

From *A Sampler of Mathematics Assessment*. Sacramento: California Department of Education, 1991.

How did I select this piece for the portfolio? How does it compare to previous work? To the work of other artists? What will I try next? Through written and oral dialogue over a series of selected pieces, students gain an understanding of the creative process and product, art history, art criticism, and aesthetics.

It is worth noting that the authentic assessment techniques described above are not reserved for high-achieving students. To the contrary, the impact of decontextualized, narrowly focused testing has been particularly devastating for students in compensatory education programs. Many of these students spend their entire school lives doing remedial exercises designed to drum in the basic skills, with the regrettable result that they never gain access to the rigorous education they need. Better options are available. Portfolio assessment offers a constructive way to meet federal requirements for eligibility to ECIA Chapter 1 programs while driving the curriculum in the direction of more challenging and interesting learning experiences. A core group of resource teachers at the elementary level in California are currently field-testing portfolio assessments in English and mathematics toward that end.

Multiple-choice Tests Versus Performance Assessment

Many educational leaders who like the idea of authentic assessment in theory are frightened away by its high front-end costs. After all, a machine can score an answer sheet a lot faster than a teacher can assess an essay. But the costs to school districts of a publisher's multiple-choice test as compared to performance assessments are like apples and oranges —not comparable. Whereas the former is a discrete budget item, the latter actually contributes to several areas of the educational enterprise. When teachers design assessment tasks and evaluate the subsequent performances of students, the experience unifies curriculum, assessment, and professional development in the most effective way imaginable. Witness the reaction of a mathematics teacher after taking part in the grading of the first CAP open-ended mathematics question in 1987:

All teachers need this experience to appreciate the misconceptions their students have! When we first read the papers, we were struck by the lack of communication—the inability of students to explain what they were doing. At first, we were defensive. We had taught these kids. We saw they were having difficulty. We had not asked them to explain, to discuss, to communicate enough. After grading these tests, we knew that we needed to stress understanding of concepts and higher level thinking in mathematics. We needed to go beyond expecting students to compute on command. We needed to expect students to be their own programmers; to be their own thinkers; to be self-sufficient in mathematics—in short, to have mathematical power.

For all the progress of recent years, however, the obstinate fact remains that norm-referenced, multiple-choice tests of basic skills continue to typify assessment in many of California's elementary schools. Most off-the-shelf test packages from publishing houses still reflect a narrow view of assessment that is heavy on mastery of the academic subskills and light on demonstrating real understanding through student performance. The recommendation of the Task Force in this area, then, is straightforward:

RECOMMENDATION

Continue building a system of authentic, performance-based assessments that measures the full scope of the thinking curriculum.

SECTION TWO
Next Steps in Authentic Assessment

California has assumed a pioneering role in the creation of an assessment system that supports the thinking curriculum. To further this work, the Task Force advances three key ideas, as reflected in recommendations 22, 23, and 24.

RECOMMENDATION

Define a set of performance standards for the elementary years.

The essence of authentic assessment is that it gives information about student progress in terms of the learning goals schools are trying to foster. The difficulty is that the state has not yet reached agreement concerning what those performance standards should be. Certainly, the latest generation of curriculum frameworks has done an admirable job of defining our expectations for student learning in general terms. However, the frameworks do not, nor should they be expected to, address the question of specific outcomes.

Properly done, performance standards—not to be confused with minimum competency levels that all students must attain—would embody California's educational goals in terms of tasks and outcomes. They would allow teachers to discuss student progress with parents and others interested in the effectiveness of the public schools in terms of what students can actually do—using student portfolios, long-term projects, and the results of on-demand performance assessments as concrete illustrations. Students

The latest generation of curriculum frameworks has done an admirable job of defining our expectations for student learning.

could be located along a graduated scale of performance levels that describe their growing achievement in narrative terms. The percent of students reaching an articulated level on a given performance standard would provide better evidence of a school's success than its percentile ranking compared with hypothetically similar schools.

Certainly, reaching a consensus on performance standards—and disseminating that information through the profession—is a large undertaking. But it is fundamental to creating a powerful statewide assessment and accountability program that supports the most ambitious goals of the thinking curriculum.

RECOMMENDATION

23 Assess limited-English-proficient (LEP) students' performance in the home language.

Current assessment practices in California were not designed with the growing language diversity of the student population in mind. As a rule, elementary LEP students are either required to take tests in English or are excluded from the assessment process. Neither practice is acceptable. Teaching students in their home language (as the Task Force recommends, where feasible), then testing them in English is a charade; excluding language-minority students from the testing process leaves out a sizable and growing portion of the student population, thereby tending to diminish the school's accountability for the success of *all* its students.

The solution to assessing the performance of LEP students is to assess their skills in the language in which they are learning. This may be costly, but the state should undertake the task immediately, beginning with the largest language groups in the student population. The Task Force recognizes the importance of primary language instruction for many LEP students. To give a fair accounting of their progress, the testing of these children should be conducted in the language of instruction.

RECOMMENDATION

24 Do not assign letter grades during the primary years.

Elementary teachers and schools should review their grading practices to determine what useful information, if any, they are communicating to parents through the use of letter grades. In general, grades shed little light on what teachers and parents most need to know to improve future learning opportunities—namely, the learning strengths and weaknesses of each student. Instead, grades tend to label students and sort and select them into *de facto* learning tracks. Especially at the kindergarten and primary level, assessment practices that promote rank ordering and diminish the self-esteem of some students should be avoided.

In place of grades, progressive teachers are learning to monitor student growth in terms of a child's placement on performance scales. At parent conferences, evaluative conversations are based on a review of a collection of the child's work samples rather than on the meaning of a sterile letter grade. Keeping a written log of each child's progress may sound time-consuming, but teachers who do so say it is an invaluable aid to their tailoring learning activities to the child's specific needs. The Primary Language Record, described in an accompanying box, offers one model for organizing a continuous narrative account of individual student progress.

The California Learning Record

The California Learning Record (CLR) is a flexible tool for analyzing the progress of students as it is revealed in their reading, writing, talking, and listening across the curriculum in English and other languages. It originated in inner London elementary schools to help teachers document their observations of what is being learned. All those who work with the child—including parents, other teachers, and, professionals—provide input. The child is invited to participate by sharing thoughts and feelings about the learning experience. The CLR provides a summary record in narrative form which documents the child's development through each school year. The audiences for this record include the parents and the child as well as the child's next-year teacher.

During the year, teachers using the CLR consult a five-point scale of descriptors of reading performance to assess the child's increasing independence as a reader in any subject area—from beginner to fluent reader. A second scale rates the child's increasing sophistication with a broad variety of reading materials—from inexperienced to experienced. Sample descriptions of the student's reading in different situations and contents as well as examples of student writing and oral language are kept with the CLR to illustrate the analyses made on the record. By determining what the child's work reveals about what the child is learning, teachers can identify which children require additional support and what form of help is most appropriate.

Early comments from teachers using the CLR include: "This is a powerful way to connect with parents." "The reading observation component truly 'makes' the observer focus on what the reader and writer can do, not on their deficits." "CLR is *the* vehicle for bringing about a paradigm shift in elementary English-language arts instruction."

In general, grades shed little light on what teachers and parents most need to know to improve future learning opportunities.

California requires assessment instruments and grading practices that elicit and record the full spectrum of rich, complex performances its citizens want students to become capable of producing. The assessment formats employed must be as inventive as the outcomes we seek to engender. A great deal of work in this field remains to be done in the next decade. The incentive to do that work is enormous, however. Perhaps no other initiative is likely to have so powerful an impact on the quality of elementary schooling as the reform of assessment and grading practices.

For Further Information

Barrs, Myra, and others. *The Primary Language Record Handbook.* Portsmouth, N.H.: Heinemann Educational Books, Inc., 1988.

Cannell, John. *Educational Measurement: Issues and Practices,* Vol. 7 (Summer, 1988), 5–9.

Cushman, Kathleen. "The Whys and Hows of the Multi-Age Primary Classroom," *American Educator,* Vol. 14, No. 2 (Summer, 1990), 28–32, 39.

"Guidelines for Appropriate Curriculum Content and Assessment in Programs Serving Children Ages 3 Through 8: A Position Statement of the National Association for the Education of Young Children and the National Association of Early Childhood Specialists in State Departments of Education," *Young Children,* (March, 1991), 21–38.

Quality Criteria for Elementary Schools: Planning, Implementing, Self-Study, and Program Quality Review. Sacramento: California Department of Education, 1989.

"Redirecting Assessment," *Educational Leadership*, Vol. 46 (April, 1989), entire issue.

Stiggins, Richard J. "Improving Assessment Where It Means the Most: In the Classroom," *Educational Leadership,* Vol. 43 (October, 1985), 69–74.

Wiggins, Grant. "A True Test: Toward More Authentic and Equitable Assessment," *Phi Delta Kappan*, Vol. 70 (May, 1989), 703–713.

Wolf, Dennie. "Portfolio Assessment: Sampling Student Work," *Educational Leadership,* Vol. 46 (April, 1989), 35–39.

CREATION OF A LEARNING ENVIRONMENT

SCHOOLS ARE LITTLE SOCIETIES THAT SUCCEED OR FAIL AS THEY ARE ABLE to enlist the energy, creativity, and drive of the people who support them in the service of broadly agreed-on educational goals. Low-performing schools that turn themselves around rarely do so as the result of a tremendous influx of new money, outside talent, or patronage. Rather, example after example suggests that schools improve when a core of teachers and concerned parents begin insisting that schools improve and when teachers and parents begin acting as a team to reinforce each other's efforts in delivering a quality education to all the students at the school site.

This commitment to excellence—to working together purposefully, respectfully, and trustingly in the pursuit of an agreed-on educational vision—is characteristic of all successful schools. Thus, the research speaks of a pervasive climate of caring and mutual support among staff and students that seems to typify a culture in exemplary schools that affirms important interpersonal and social values by modeling them in action. As abstract as such concepts may seem, they are absolutely crucial to supporting the learning and growth of *all* students. The purpose of this chapter is to focus on the human dynamic of change at the school site.

Important First Steps

RECOMMENDATION

25 **Develop a unifying vision of what the school is trying to accomplish.**

In successful elementary schools, the staff, parents, and community have articulated a common vision of what the school is trying to accomplish. The process of creating a vision should begin by gathering information from both within the immediate school community and beyond. Locally, through questionnaires, formal meetings, and less-formal conversations, faculty, staff, parents, students, local citizens, and businesspeople have opportunities to be heard. In establishing a vision of what is possible, school staff should also scan the educational horizon beyond the school. Reading the reports of research, visiting other schools, and consulting curriculum experts are all necessary steps in the investigative process.

Gathering all the available information and then developing a vision for the school are formidable tasks. Whatever techniques are used for reaching a consensus and establishing a vision, the most important thing to bear in mind is to keep the process open! The ongoing process of developing a unifying vision helps promote a sense of belonging and community among all those who take part. Staff members feel supported, appreciated, and respected as members of the school team. This feeling, in turn, encourages a continuing willingness to take part in the renewal process.

RECOMMENDATION

26 **Use the vision of the school as a guide for action.**

As important an exercise as the articulation of a school's vision is, the real power of a clearly stated vision comes when it is used to guide improvement efforts at the school. All too often schools view the creation of a shared vision as an end in itself. Once the vision is agreed on, it is sent home in written form to parents and plastered on bookcovers and bulletin boards, soon becoming part of the background rather than the focal point for ongoing discussions and the design of improvement initiatives at the school.

Even when members of the school community intend to use the vision statement as a guide for action, their efforts are often blunted by the idea of developing a school improvement plan. Squirreled away in closets and hidden on the uppermost bookshelf in many of California's elementary schools, school plans often become monuments to the planning process rather than useful documents. But how could it be otherwise? Change is a

Portrait of a 'Turnaround School'

Hawthorne Elementary School in San Francisco's Mission District is a California Distinguished School. By any standard of comparison, the recognition is well-deserved: its 99-percent-plus attendance rate, the upbeat staff, and positive student attitudes are evident the moment you walk through the school's doors. Serving a population of mainly poor minority children, Hawthorne is a school that works—that succeeds in providing each of its students a challenging and worthwhile education. And yet, teachers there will tell you they can remember a time not so long ago when Hawthorne was a "place on the other side of time"—a place in which the majority of children did not learn; in which bullies raced down hallways on bicycles, out of control; and in which the cardinal rule of professional survival was "keep your problems to yourself."

How did the dramatic turnaround at Hawthorne come about? Teachers, parents, and a committed principal made it happen by working together and by refusing to give up on a single child. The coalition started with a symbolic and practical victory: pushing the school district to rehabilitate the building. Today, beautiful murals by neighborhood artists have replaced the profanity that once decorated the school's exterior walls. A schoolwide disciplinary policy based on mutual respect was agreed on, ensuring that halls and playgrounds were safe and pleasant places to be.

Seizing on the momentum created by the changed atmosphere, the school began a vision-setting process. Over 90 percent of the 700 students on site are linguistically and/or dialectically distinct from the English-speaking majority. Granted this fact, Hawthorne's faculty decided to make the language development of students its number one priority through both English and native language development, daily integrated reading instruction in grades two through five, and oral language instruction targeted to the child's language background three times a week.

Recognizing the full extent of their roles as primary teachers, Hawthorne's faculty reached out to parents, contacting them with good news, not just bad; holding meetings in their neighborhoods (many children are bused to the school); and publishing a weekly *Parent Bulletin* in three languages. Today, the parents' group has a wider base of support and involvement than ever before. The school library has been expanded to include a significant number of native-language titles. In place of teacher isolation, the faculty now meets regularly, both by grade level and as a whole, to discuss educational issues, plan schoolwide curricular programs, and set goals.

"The learning environment needs to provide stability and familiarity; this is part of the function of routine classroom behaviors and procedures. At the same time, provision must be made to satisfy our hunger for novelty, discovery, and challenge."

Renate N. Caine and Geoffrey Caine[1]

dynamic process. A document that pretends to settle once and for all the changes needed seems doomed at the outset.

How then do schools proceed? The Task Force suggests that schools acknowledge change as a dynamic process and redefine the notion of a school plan. Holding the vision constant, members of the school community should consider as their "improvement plan" the ongoing record of agreements as the next step to be taken to improve the school. For example, one section of the plan might include more formal statements of goals and activities resulting from strategic planning sessions, while another section might record the on-site visits by teacher-leaders who help the school's leadership team take concrete best-next-steps toward curricular improvement. The plan, kept in a looseleaf notebook, allows for additions to be inserted as needed. Accumulated minutes of staff and school site council meetings can be added when it is appropriate. Such a plan is superior to the traditional improvement plan in two ways. First, it allows flexibility in

The plan, kept in a looseleaf notebook, allows for additions to be inserted as needed.

A Comprehensive Approach to Character Education

If a school wishes to maximize its impact on the values of students, it must have a vision that sees the moral significance of all aspects of schooling and uses all phases of classroom and school life to foster character development.

"Within the classroom, a comprehensive approach calls upon *the teacher* to:

1. **Act as caregiver, model, and mentor,** treating students with love and respect, setting a good example, supporting pro-social behavior, and correcting hurtful actions.
2. **Create a moral community in the classroom,** helping students know each other, respect and care about each other, and feel valued membership in the group.
3. **Practice moral discipline,** using the creation and enforcement of rules as opportunities to foster moral reasoning, self-control, and a generalized respect for others.
4. **Create a democratic classroom environment,** involving students in decision-making and shared responsibility for making the classroom a good place to be and to learn.
5. **Teach values through the curriculum,** using academic subjects as a vehicle for examining ethical issues. (This is simultaneously a schoolwide strategy when the curriculum addresses cross-grade concerns such as sex, drug, and alcohol education.)
6. **Use cooperative learning** to teach children the disposition and skills of helping each other and working together.

meeting the needs for change at the school. Second, it allows all members of the school community to join the change process at any time. Nothing is more off-putting to interested parents or enthusiastic new teachers than to be told their ideas are wonderful but they will have to wait until the school plan is revised next May.

For Further Information

Comer, James P. "New Haven's School-Community Connection," *Educational Leadership,* Vol. 44 (March, 1987), 13–16.

Comer, James P. "Educating Poor Minority Children," *Scientific American*, Vol. 259, No. 5 (November, 1988), 42–48.

Schaps, Eric, and Daniel Solomon. "Schools and Classrooms as Caring Communities," *Educational Leadership*, Vol. 48 (November, 1990), 38–42.

Creating a Caring School Community: Ideas from the Child Development Project. San Ramon, Calif.: Developmental Studies Center, 1989.

7. **Develop the 'conscience of craft' by** fostering students' academic responsibility and their regard for the value of learning and work.

8. **Encourage moral reflection** through reading, writing, discussion, decision-making exercises, and debate.

9. **Teach conflict resolution** so that students have the capacity and commitment to solve conflicts in fair, nonviolent ways.

"A comprehensive approach calls upon *the school* to:

10. **Foster caring beyond the classroom,** using inspiring role models and opportunities for school and community service to help students learn to care by giving care.

11. **Create a positive moral culture in the school,** developing a total school environment (through the leadership of the principal, schoolwide discipline, a schoolwide sense of community, democratic student government, a moral community among adults, and time for addressing moral concerns) that supports and amplifies the values taught in classrooms.

12. **Recruit parents and the community as partners in values education,** supporting parents as the child's first moral teacher; encouraging parents to support the school in its efforts to foster good values; and seeking the help of the community (e.g., churches, business, and the media) in reinforcing the values the school is trying to teach."

Quoted and reprinted with permission from *Educating for Character: How Our Schools Can Teach Respect and Responsibility* by Thomas Lickona. New York: Bantam Books, Inc., 1991. © 1991 by Dr. Thomas Lickona.

Experienced elementary teachers know that good instructional practices and the attentive participation of their students go hand in hand.

RECOMMENDATION

27 **Bond students to their schools by making them feel part of a caring community.**

In exemplary elementary schools, children feel a palpable sense of belonging—of being part of a friendly neighborhood of welcoming adults and peers who care about one another's feelings and aspirations and who support one another's social, intellectual, and emotional growth. Schools can promote such a nurturing atmosphere through various strategies:

1. Recognize students and their scholarly efforts in assemblies and recitals, on bulletin board displays, in newsletters, and in other ways. Such recognition helps build self-esteem and a common dedication to learning and provides children incentives for continuing to do well in the future.

2. Use the home language of LEP students in "official" settings, such as school newsletters, announcements, and assemblies. For students from diverse cultures, hearing or seeing their language and traditions represented in school-wide contexts shows an appreciation for who they are and sends an important message of inclusion. This celebration of diversity should grow out of and reflect the school's underlying rhythms, however, and not simply be reserved for special events.

3. Give students a chance to give back to others as well as receive. Schools can create occasions for students to show their helpfulness in many ways: collecting canned goods in food drives for the homeless at Thanksgiving; adopting a local senior citizen's home for regular visits, or beautifying a corner of the school yard in the spring. By sponsoring group participation in such unselfish deeds and recognizing the participants, the school community affirms the significant values for which it stands.

For Further Information

Conrad, Dan and Diane Hedin. *Youth Service: A Guidebook for Developing and Operating Effective Programs.* Washington, D.C.: Independent Sector, 1987.

Grant, Gerald. "The Character of Education and the Education of Character," *Daedalus*, Vol. 110 (summer, 1981), 135–149.

Wayson, William W., and others. *Handbook for Developing Schools with Good Discipline.* Bloomington, Ind.: Phi Delta Kappa Commission on Discipline, 1982.

Schools can create occasions for students to show their helpfulness in many ways.

RECOMMENDATION

28 **Reach out to parents to solicit their active involvement in the education of their children.**

The research regarding the effect of parental involvement on the education of young children is both well-known and unequivocal. Such involvement helps motivate students, particularly those from low-income households, and has a marked positive impact on their achievement. Unfortunately, parental involvement remains a largely underutilized resource in promoting improved learning outcomes. Parents may hesitate to become active in their child's education for a variety of reasons, including their hectic schedules, a lack of awareness of the importance of such participation, a feeling that educators are the experts in this arena, or even an aversion to the institution stemming from their own educational experiences.

Whatever has prevented parents from becoming involved in their children's education, the antidote is clear. The most important variable in determining whether parents become involved in their children's education is not family size, marital status, or level of education attained; rather, it is the school's program itself. When schools pursue a comprehensive program of involving parents in all facets of the educational endeavor, parents respond enthusiastically and their children greatly benefit. The program may include any or all of the following activities:

- Helping parents develop their parenting skills
- Coordinating community support services on the behalf of parents

The Invisible Curriculum

The invisible curriculum consists of all the messages that adults send to children about what is valued and respected in the adult world. These messages are critical for shaping the character of children, their outlook on life, and their ability to interact effectively with others. The content of the invisible curriculum helps teach children how much value to place on themselves and others. It develops and reinforces good habits, shared values, and high standards of behavior, all of which are likely to produce adults who succeed in education and in life.

An effective invisible curriculum stresses, among other things, good work habits, teamwork, perseverance, honesty, self-reliance, and consideration for others. These "character builders" are as important to future success in the workplace and in life as the academic skills taught through the regular curriculum and should be stressed in the home as well as in school.

Quoted from *The Unfinished Agenda: A New Vision for Child Development and Education.* A statement by the Research and Policy Committee of the Committee for Economic Development. New York: Committee for Economic Development, 1991, p. 55. Reprinted by permission.

- Informing parents how best to assist their children in learning at home
- Promoting clear two-way communication regarding their child's progress
- Involving volunteer parents in support roles at school to help lower the adult:student ratio
- Soliciting parents to serve as informed decision makers in governance, advisory, and school advocacy roles

Many approaches can be taken to involve parents in the education of their children in the various capacities listed above:

1. An obvious starting point is to invite parents to participate and to make them feel welcome when they accept. An introductory letter from the teacher to the parents at the beginning of the year helps establish rapport and starts the year on a positive note; answering telephone calls from parents on the same day they are received helps to maintain good relations. Personally inviting parents to eat lunch with their children at school or to observe their children in the classroom whenever they are able to are also positive actions a teacher can take.

2. Teachers should meet with parents individually at the beginning of

Family Homework

Short homework assignments designed to stretch elementary students' thinking while helping busy families spend enjoyable time together have been standard fare in the San Ramon School District since 1985. Typically, teachers send home assignments every two or three weeks that involve families in reading short stories or poems drawn from the best of children's literature. The stories poignantly or humorously illustrate common family conflicts. Children answer questions about the reading selection, and an accompanying discussion guide suggests ways for their parents to go beyond the reading to talk with their children more generally about the issues and values the selection raises.

For example, third graders have gone home with a chapter from *The Stories Julian Tells* in which Julian and his little brother Huey eat the special pudding their father has made for their mother. With mock severity, their father devises a "punishment" that means "some 'whipping' and some 'beating' around here" —the kind involved when the boys help cook a new pudding to replace the one they ate. This Family Homework assignment modeled a positive disciplinary strategy, illustrated typical childhood (mis)behavior, and provided an opportunity to discuss similar problems at home.

the school year, rather than waiting until scheduled conferences when the agenda is to review a student's progress. The purpose of this initial meeting is for the teacher to learn about the student's interests, hobbies, languages spoken, previous school experiences, and so forth. Collecting such information early from parents not only allows the teacher to devise strategies to connect child and curriculum but also forcefully communicates to parents the school's interest and concern for each student.

3. Schools can publish newsletters in which the contributions of parents, students, and staff are saluted on a regular basis.

4. Parents can be made more familiar with the curriculum through students' performances, such as science fairs, mathematics games, historical dramas, or physical fitness demonstrations.

5. Parent-teacher conferences should be scheduled at times convenient to working parents, including before school, during lunch, or in the evenings. In school districts desegregated by busing, parent conferences conducted in English as well as an appropriate native language can be held in school buildings in the neighborhoods from which the students have been transported. This makes it convenient for parents or guardians to attend, and it increases participation.

An introductory letter from the teacher to the parents at the beginning of the year helps establish rapport.

Reaction to the Family Homework approach has been overwhelmingly favorable. "My son loved the story," one mother wrote of the Julian assignment. "He told me the father's reaction was much better than sending the boys to their room or spanking them. I learned something too. I hope I can have patience, as Julian's father had. It helps to have reminders sometimes."

Another parent agreed: "With everything so hectic, there never seems to be enough time. But with Family Homework, even though I keep saying 'I don't have the time,' somehow I find 10 minutes to sit down and spend the time. Once you sit down and begin, it turns into fun. Even when it stretches into 45 minutes, I've learned about my son as a person. Instead of the usual 'what did you do in school today?' Family Homework lets me discover the inside part of him."

Teachers support Family Homework because "It's not just busywork," one third-grade teacher commented. "The selections are well thought out and they help families look at their own systems of values by stimulating discussions." Indeed, a kindergarten teacher found her parents asking for more frequent Family Homework assignments!

Adapted from *Working Together*, newsletter of the Child Development Project. Summer, 1986, Number 14.

A direct way for an elementary school to break down old, inherited psychological barriers of unapproachability is to physically open itself up, before and after school, to respond to the community's needs. From early in the morning to late at night, on weekends and during the summer, the school can be the locus for child care services by third-party providers, for community meetings, and for continuing education classes. Depending on the interests and needs of its community, the school can provide parent education courses with a variety of emphases. Topics might include how to cope with temper tantrums, how to teach children responsibility, or how to promote the child's self-esteem. At Foster Road Elementary School in Norwalk-La Mirada, a library of "video outreach" tapes in English and Spanish has been amassed for parents' use with a standard VCR. This approach allows parents to choose instructional topics particularly relevant to their own needs and to review them at their convenience.

The most important way in which parents can support their children's learning is with assistance at home. Helping with homework allows parents to see how well their children are progressing in school. Furthermore, it communicates directly to the child the importance the family places on doing well in school. The parent's traditional role in helping with homework is largely organizational: seeing to it that the child has a quiet, well-lit place to work; setting aside a regular time for doing homework; reviewing what has been assigned and developing a schedule for completing it; and providing encouragement and praise when the job is done. In leading elementary schools, however, the concept of homework itself is changing and making room for more sophisticated interactions between parent and child. Consistent with the philosophy of the thinking curriculum, homework is no longer regarded solely as an occasion for extended skills-based practice; rather, more and more assignments are providing open-ended opportunities for meaningful work that challenges students to think, reason, and apply skills to specific situations. Thought-provoking "family" homework assignments, such as talking over a reading selection that deals with a common parent/child conflict or writing down the story of how the family came to California, have proved highly popular with parents when they have been tried.

The most important way in which parents can support their children's learning is with assistance at home.

For Further Information

Berliner, D., and U. Casanova. "Is Parent Involvement Worth the Effort?" *Instructor* (October, 1985), 20–21.

The Changing History–Social Science Curriculum, A Booklet for Parents. Sacramento: California Department of Education, 1990.

The Changing Language Arts Curriculum, A Booklet for Parents. Sacramento: California Department of Education, 1990. (Available in English and Spanish.)

The Changing Mathematics Curriculum, A Booklet for Parents. Sacramento: California Department of Education, 1989. (Available in English and Spanish.)

Cooper, Harris. "Synthesis of Research on Homework," *Educational Leadership,*
Vol. 47 (November, 1989), 85–91.

Epstein, J. "Parents' Reactions to Teacher Practices of Parent Involvement,"
Elementary School Journal, Vol. 86 (January, 1989), 277–294.

"Strengthening Partnerships with Parents and Community," *Educational Leadership,* Vol. 47 (October, 1989), entire issue.

RECOMMENDATION

29 **Systematically upgrade school plants statewide.**

Another step to creating an environment conducive to learning is
establishing a school setting that is safe and welcoming with physical
facilities that support the growth of *all* students. The business world
knows that if you put people in a clean, well-lighted, attractive workplace,
they not only have a brighter outlook but also tend to produce more as well.
Schools need to act on this insight. Unfortunately, deferred capital spending
on maintenance has begun to manifest itself in the older elementary school
facilities in the state in a big way. Too often, boilers don't work, carpets are
worn out, lavatories are poorly maintained, and the school setting as a
whole communicates a message of neglect and lack of pride.

In schools that work, the physical environment is clean, pleasant, and well-maintained.

While many of the decisions on maintenance are made elsewhere, a
great deal can still be done at the local level. In schools that work, the
physical environment is clean, pleasant, and well-maintained. Furniture and
space are functional and adaptable to the frequent regrouping of students
according to the particular demands of a given learning activity. Adequate
room is dedicated for drama, dance, physical education, music, and other
classes with special space requirements. The reading program is supported
by a wealth of print and non-print materials, both in the classroom and in a
school-wide library. Reading materials in the library reflect the variety of
home languages spoken by students in the school. The media center is rich
with technology, hands-on materials, and other resources to stimulate
student learning. The nutrition program is supported by a cafeteria that has
adequate space for all children to eat, and adequate time is allocated
through proper scheduling so that students have an opportunity to read or to
spend quiet time before and after the meal.

Of course, the caring school community provides not just a physical
safe haven for students but also a psychological one. Students know that
they are protected at school—from the random violence they may have
observed elsewhere in their lives or from any other threat to their security.
For instance, it is estimated that as many as half of the foreign born in
California are here without documentation. High correlations exist between
undocumented status and dropping out or never enrolling in school. According to *Crossing the Schoolhouse Border,* ". . . occasional INS raids on

Food for Thought

Part of creating a healthy learning environment is providing good examples in deed as well as in theory. Montebello Unified School District's nutrition program embraces this philosophy in several ways. First, because good eating habits are acquired early in life, the food offered in the school lunch program exemplifies principles of good nutritional choice, including the use of whole grains in all baked products; daily offerings of fresh fruits or vegetables; a reduction in fats, salts, and sugar (french fries are baked, with no decrease in their tremendous popularity); a decrease in serving of processed meats and hot dogs; and increased servings of poultry, fish, beans, salads, and nonfat milk. Second, since children learn best by doing, three times per year each elementary school has a "student menu day" in which students choose the menu, subject to some budgetary restrictions, of course. This provides a concrete opportunity to teach nutrition, discuss the lunch program, and explain the notion of a well-balanced meal. In addition, managers offer tours of the kitchen, allowing students some hands-on activities, such as scooping cookies (which they later eat). Throughout the year, Montebello's menus have custom-made backs, with information tailored to be understood by young students and their parents. By moving from the classroom to the lunchroom, Montebello has demonstrated how to bolster important lessons in good health with the kind of delicious reinforcements children are likely to remember.

school sites, the use of children as 'bait' to entrap undocumented adults, and ignorance or outright breaking of policy by school staff and authorities who ask for immigration papers as a condition of registration. . ." have all exacerbated children's fears of the school environment.[2] Children of all ethnic groups and cultural heritages need to be reassured that schools not only guarantee them a safe environment, free from prejudice and harassment, but also that the school setting is an inclusive and welcoming one that celebrates the diversity of its various members.

For Further Information

Comer, James P. "New Haven's School-Community Connection," *Educational Leadership,* Vol. 44 (March, 1987), 13–16.

What Works: Research About Teaching and Learning. Washington, D.C.: U.S. Department of Education, 1987.

Kohn, Alfie. "The ABC's of Caring," *Teacher Magazine* (January, 1990), 52–58.

Not Schools Alone: Guidelines for Schools and Communities to Prevent the Use of Tobacco, Alcohol, and Other Drugs Among Children and Youth. Sacramento: California Department of Education, 1991.

Schools for the Twenty-first Century. Sacramento: California Department of Education, 1991.

COORDINATING STUDENT SERVICES

CHILDREN HAVE CERTAIN PHYSICAL AND EMOTIONAL SECURITY NEEDS that must be met before they are free to concern themselves with anything else, including doing well in school. At a minimum, children need to know that food, clothing, and shelter will be provided reliably and that they will be properly cared for when sick. No less eagerly, however, children also seek the validation and emotional support of significant adults in their lives—be it in the form of a word of praise, a few minutes of undivided attention, or a hug. Unfortunately, as was noted in the Introduction to this report, an increasing number of children are coming to school without these basic needs having been satisfied. Some neglected children require intensive, immediate help. But being "at risk" in these stressful times is not a static concept. Virtually every child will experience anxieties and emotional difficulties outside school at some point in his or her upbringing. The purpose of this chapter is to map out a coherent strategy for the early recognition and resolution of extracurricular problems, based on a philosophy of risk prevention and on a vision of the schools as a hub for a coordinated multiagency response.

The Problem of Fragmentation

The debate over how much responsibility the schools should assume in addressing underlying social problems is a long-standing one. Earlier this century, the innovation of hot lunch programs was roundly criticized as an unnecessary frill that would detract from the essential academic mission of the schools. The evident difficulty of teaching hungry students eventually won out in that argument. But today, parallel misgivings have emerged regarding the appropriateness of providing basic health services, psychological counseling, or social services at the school site in an era of limited educational funds. In reality, hunger is a statewide problem with one out of three children needing our immediate attention. In a recent report, "The Community Childhood Hunger Identification Project," it was estimated that 647,000 children in California are hungry, and an additional 725,0000 are on the brink of hunger.[1] The lack of breakfast programs is a serious problem, with only 33 percent of the children currently receiving free or reduced-price school lunches also eating school breakfasts.

Research studies have documented that many American children are malnourished and consume diets that are nutritionally inadequate. Although physical symptoms of malnourished children may not be obvious, such children are likely to demonstrate behavioral abnormalities, such as shortened attention spans and lack of motivation, motor insufficiencies, and diminished sensory integration. Undernutrition increases the risk and severity of illlnesses, and iron deficiency anemia results in shortened attention span, fatigue, and decreased ability to concentrate. Anemic children do poorly on vocabulary, reading, mathematics, problem solving, and psychological tests. Consequently, it is important that schools attempt to do their part in meeting the nutritional needs of our children. By providing balanced meals through the School Breakfast Program and National School Lunch Program, schools can play a major role in meeting such needs.

The number and extent of social problems children bring to school have grown rapidly, but solutions to these problems are slow in coming. In addressing children's issues, the nonpartisan statewide organization, Children Now, gave California an overall "D" grade—seriously deficient—for the well-being of its youngest generation as measured by 27 statistical indicators, including immunization, foster care, infant mortality, homelessness, and so on.[2]

Obviously, the schools by themselves cannot remedy all the problems that children face in society. No less than 160 state programs located in seven departments and run by 37 state units have been authorized to serve children and youth in California.[3] As many recent reports have pointed out, however, a direct result of this jerry-rigged structure is that the programs sometimes function in a fragmented, duplicative, and reactive manner. Usually, a state program operates in a targeted area that is aimed at a narrow aspect of a family's problems: domestic violence, illiteracy, alcoholism, child abuse, unemployment. A child and parent might come in contact with a half dozen social service agencies, ranging from county welfare, child protective services, and Medicaid to mental health or the juvenile courts, yet never find a counselor truly committed to cutting through the knot of underlying problems to provide the needed services. Rarely are services to children and their families provided in a comprehensive, continuing, and coordinated fashion. The focus is on crisis intervention instead of on prevention—on pieces of the problem instead of on the healthfulness of the whole child.

Traditionally, school programs aimed at fostering the well-being of children have suffered from defects similar to the ones existing at the state level: being fragmented and too narrow in conception. For example, the schools have tended to target such health risks as drunk driving, AIDS, teenage pregnancy, suicide, or drug, alcohol, and tobacco abuse with ad-hoc

Traditionally, school programs aimed at fostering the well-being of children have suffered from a similar defect of being fragmented and too narrow in conception.

Educating Drug-Damaged Children

One of the tragic legacies of the explosion in the use of crack cocaine in the United States in the mid-to-late 1980s is a wave of children who were born addicted to drugs. Those children will be entering elementary school in the 1990s. Educating these children poses a number of challenges. The range of effects of substance exposure prenatally can go from no discernible interference with cognitive or social development to severe impairment, neurologically and emotionally. For some children, the neurological damage they have sustained manifests itself in abrupt mood swings, short attention spans, and difficulty in developing attachments to teachers and classmates. Some are hyperactive and easily overwhelmed by new stimuli. Some have language problems.

The Salvin Special Education Center in Los Angeles, a pilot program run by teachers and UCLA pediatricians, has pioneered educational strategies for helping drug-exposed children overcome these problems. Techniques developed there are being disseminated to other Los Angeles area elementary schools. Nurturing care and individual attention are the main elements in the Salvin program, which has recorded some gratifying successes. At $15,000 per student per year, however, the approach is expensive and underlines a truism about coping with social problems: prevention is the best medicine.

informational campaigns offered in the high school years. But research has clearly demonstrated that such knowledge-based programs do not change the incidence of self-destructive behaviors. These programs have failed because they ignored the fact that students decide to engage in such behaviors by responding to emotion rather than intellect. Their emotions are shaped over the years by the combined influences of family, peers, school, and community.

Learning from this experience, educators have started to "immunize" children against unhealthy risk-taking behaviors by using a two-component approach. The first element consists of a comprehensive health education program beginning in the early grades (when students are still receptive to the message) that puts an emphasis on wellness as a life-style. The second element seeks to improve the external climate by reaching out to each of the important influence groups in the child's life to form protective partnerships that advocate for good health habits.

In their separate spheres, then, both educators and human service professionals have come to the same conclusion: new alliances must be formed to allow all children to reach their full physical, mental, and emotional potential. Schools alone cannot succeed in this task. The influence of family, community, and peers is too important to ignore. Nor can individual agencies with their narrowly aimed programs make a lasting difference. The emphasis needs to be on working together and treating the whole child. Toward that end, human service agencies in several counties in California—Napa, San Bernardino, San Mateo, Santa Clara, Santa Cruz, Solano, and Stanilaus, for example—have formed collaborative networks that are regarded as national models of how to successfully pool resources and jointly solve problems rather than allocate services according to some rigid definition.

SECTION TWO

Meeting the Physical and Security Needs of Children

While a holistic approach to solving complex family problems is proving productive in some locales, it will also require state-level leadership so that districts and counties do not have to keep reinventing the wheel at the local level. This process has already begun. The Healthy Start Support Services for Children Act (Senate Bill 620) is the cornerstone of recent initiatives targeted at prevention and early intervention programs for children in California. This legislation provides funds to school districts and counties for the purpose of coordinating services for children and their families at or near school sites. The goal of this initiative is to ensure that students, especially those at-risk, have access to the health, mental health, and social services and other progams that they need to succeed in school and to improve their health and psycho-social outcomes.

The ultimate goal of SB 620 is the establishment of a comprehensive, statewide system of school-linked services for children and their families. Underlying this ambitious goal is the belief that children who come to school ill, hungry, or neglected are not likely to be active participants in a rigorous curriculum and that the school site is the logical place where services designed to help these students and families should come together. Because schools are conveniently located and are where at-risk students can be identified, they are the obvious sites for "one-stop shopping" for the special support and programs many students and their families need.

Central to a rationalized statewide human services policy is the principle of consistently investing in the prevention of health problems. All available evidence indicates that such an approach, in addition to necessary acute intervention, is the wisest strategy—educationally, socially, and financially. For instance, a few dollars spent in decreasing the incidence of low-birth-weight babies by ensuring adequate nutrition during pregnancy translates directly into many thousands of dollars saved in special education costs for children later on. A classroom full of children in a Head Start Program costs society less per annum than maintaining a single prisoner in jail for a year.

A few dollars spent in decreasing the incidence of low-birth-weight babies by ensuring adequate nutrition during pregnancy translates directly into many thousands of dollars saved in special education costs for children later on.

RECOMMENDATION

30 **Coordinate human services at the school site to ensure that the basic security needs of children are being met.**

Every school district and school can take three steps to participate in the new collaborative social services approach:

1. *Provide a setting.* The schools already have the children under one roof. That puts them in an excellent position to furnish a venue for a variety of services that can be provided by other governmental and private agencies. For example, in the Santa Clara County Inter-agency Project in San Jose, elementary schools have arranged for daily access to children of troubled families by counselors from a variety of agencies. In other elementary schools, dental, eye, and health screening clinics have all been provided on a routine basis.

2. *Designate a coordinator.* According to the PACE report, *Conditions of Children in California*, "School staff are notoriously unaware of services available through juvenile justice, social service, or mental health agencies."[4] A direct remedy for this short-coming is to designate an individual at each school site to be

responsible for maintaining linkages with community service providers. Depending on local conditions, this person might be the school nurse, a health educator, counselor, school psychologist, or lead teacher. The duties of this person should include taking part in all student study team meetings, thus making available to the action group a broad knowledge of the full menu of social service aids available on behalf of the child and child's family. The district's role in this context is to make initial contact with human service agencies and other providers and pave the way for more extensive interaction at the school site.

3. *Participate in existing efforts.* Taking part in the California Department of Education's continuing "Healthy Kids, Healthy California" initiative is one way to promote collaboration in providing services. The initiative has eight components: K–12 health education, K–12 physical education, health services for students, health promotion for staff, nutrition services, counseling support, safe and healthy

On Elementary School Counselors

Studies of child development indicate that children establish lifelong behavioral patterns from ages six through ten—the first four years of school. Elementary school counseling can have a significant influence on a student's achievement, mental health, positive self-concept, and subsequent school success during this critical juncture.

Elementary students tend to be more emotionally dependent on their teachers and parents than high school students are; more influenced by family culture than by their peers; and more limited in their abilities to make decisions and to be self-directed. An elementary school counseling program responds to these differences. For example, the elementary counselor advocates for prevention and early detection of learning problems rather than remediation; works closely with the significant adults in a child's life, especially teachers and parents; focuses more on the present problems than plans for the future; and helps students to understand themselves, learn, and live and work harmoniously with others.

Unfortunately, the elementary school counselor is a rarity. Three-quarters of California's students are enrolled in kindergarten through grade eight, but fewer than a quarter of all school counselors work at that level. Ideally, a credentialed counselor would be on staff at every elementary school. The point is that counseling is important, and the lack of a credentialed counselor does not dispense the obligation to provide adult guidance to elementary schoolchildren.

Head Start on Kindergarten

A national education goal is to ensure that by the year 2000 all children in the United States start school ready to learn. Toward that end, elementary schools and Head Start Programs are being asked to better coordinate their efforts.[5] Suggested activities include:

- *Transmit information.* Health records, data on diagnosed disabilities, developmental status, and social services received should all be provided to the child's new teacher.
- *Stage meetings.* Head Start and elementary school teachers should meet to discuss the needs and interests of each incoming child.
- *Parental involvement.* Exchange information with parents on mutual expectations for a child's school success. Welcome parents to the new school; involve them and preschool children in several activities at the school in the year prior to enrollment.
- *Lines of responsibility.* Appoint a staff member at the school site to be responsible for coordinating such collaborations.

school environment, and parent involvement. A goal of the initiative is to have campuses free of drugs, alcohol, and tobacco in California by 1996. In reaching this goal, however, the initiative recognizes the importance of reaching out to the various influence groups—community, families, schools, and peers—who help shape adolescents' decisions. The initiative's guidelines call for schools to establish formal partnerships with parents, community leaders, and local social service and law enforcement agencies in the formation of school-community risk-prevention planning teams.

Another initiative of the California Department of Education, "Every Student Succeeds," is aimed at ensuring that the needs of at-risk students are met by the schools. It, too, emphasizes the importance of establishing strong parent-community linkages, the coordinating of health and social services, and the streamlining of educational services within the school, especially in the creative use of categorical program resources.

A common misconception about schools becoming involved in addressing underlying social problems that have precluded student success is that they may lose sight of their primary mission. Making certain that needy children and their families receive a broad spectrum of prevention-oriented human services is not a goal in and of itself for schools, but rather a means to the end of providing a challenging education for every child. Coordinating support does not mean that the schools actually provide the services or even function in an administrative capacity. Rather, the idea is that the schools act in a new role as advocates for youth in building partnerships with health and human services agencies and improving the accessibility of services. Furthermore, it bears repeating that the intent of the schools, as well as social service agencies, should always be to work through families, not around them, in helping children. The role of the family is paramount in each child's development. Districts and schools can and should take the initiative in forming positive relationships with parents and other family members. Parents want to support the mission of the schools and will do so most effectively when they are involved in a decision-making partnership with the local school.

One particularly effective means for enhancing parent interest is through adult education programs. Many California school districts have used such programs to link parent education, citizenship training, ESL services, and vocational training to the ongoing programs provided to children. Head Start is another program that ties together parent education, preschool education, and health and nutrition programs in a comprehensive plan to strengthen the family unit and improve long-range educational outcomes.

In sum, elementary schools are uniquely positioned to make a difference for all children. Rather than adding to the burden of an already beleaguered profession, the Elementary Grades Task Force's recommendations should be viewed as an effort to assist schools in working with human services agencies to provide a wellness foundation for effective education. Institutionally, schools can provide the continuity of contact over time that ad hoc interventions so conspicuously lack. In collaboration with other social service providers, the elementary schools can serve as a clearinghouse for providing help to children and their families.

> Parents want to support the mission of the schools and will do so most effectively when they are involved in a decision-making partnership with the local school.

For Further Information

Chang, H. N., and others. *Fighting Fragmentation: Collaborative Efforts to Serve Children and Families in California's Counties.* San Francisco: California Tomorrow, 1991.

Every Student Succeeds. Sacramento: California Department of Education, 1990.

Gardner, Sid. "Failure by Fragmentation," *California Tomorrow,* Vol. 4 (fall, 1989), 18–25.

Hodgkinson, Harold. *The Same Client: The Demographics of Education and Service Delivery Systems.* Washington, D.C.: Institute for Educational Leadership, Inc., Center for Demographic Policy, 1989.

"Helping Youngsters Cope with Life," *Educational Leadership*, Vol. 45 (March, 1988), entire issue.

Kirst, Michael W. "Improving Children's Services," *Phi Delta Kappan* (April, 1991), 615–618.

Not Schools Alone: Guidelines for Schools and Communities to Prevent the Use of Tobacco, Alcohol, and Other Drugs Among Children and Youth. Sacramento: California Department of Education, 1990.

ORGANIZING TO MEET THE CHALLENGE

GRASSROOTS ENTHUSIASM BY ITSELF CANNOT SUSTAIN THE PROGRESS OF educational reform. In his landmark study of the school change process, Michael Fullan found that major initiatives had a fighting chance when they were supported by strong district-level leadership.[1] Without such leadership new programs and practices rarely penetrated beyond the odd classroom or school—and tended to die out completely when the individuals responsible for pushing them switched jobs or left the system.

The previous chapters of *It's Elementary!* have been directed at the local school community of teachers, parents, and site administrators. This final chapter is aimed at superintendents, district administrators, and school board members and describes the crucial role they have in improving California's elementary schools.

The New School District

The role of the school district is changing. The old industrial model of district governance put the accent on control and standardization. Teachers were implicitly regarded as assembly-line workers whose job it was to produce educated students according to a rigidly specified instructional program. Centrally planned decisions often determined everything from the length of the school day to what materials would be used in the classroom. District staff were seen as the enforcers of a myriad of rules and regulations that emanated from Washington, D.C., Sacramento, and "downtown." The problem with this model, of course, was that it stifled individual initiative and eventually led to a sterile formalism in which everyone did his or her job, but no one took final responsibility for making sure that every child received a quality education. Top-down management was never a particularly effective way to run the learning enterprise. At a time when schools are expected to teach a more demanding curriculum to a more diverse student population, management from above has become as obsolete as the smokestack industries that popularized it.

The new model of district governance takes its cue from the effective business literature of the 1980s. For example, in their book, *In Search of Excellence: Lessons from America's Best Run Companies*, Thomas J. Peters and Robert H. Waterman, Jr., analyzed how chief executive officers from some of America's most successful companies mobilized their corporate teams. Typically, these top executives led by constantly refocusing organizational attention on long-term strategic goals. As for specific tactics, however, successful chief executive officers generally left it up to local managers and workers to sort out the operational details. Ceding a substantial measure of autonomy to the grass roots was the most efficient way to get the job done.[2]

Progressive school districts have been changing their administrative approach based on the insight they have gained from the business world. The general thrust of the change—an integral part of the restructuring movement—is to tap the energy and creativity of the professional staff at the school site to achieve outstanding results. Thus, instead of constantly monitoring for compliance with rules and regulations, the district staff's main role is to enable and facilitate—to build up the capacity of people at the school site to reach agreed-on educational goals.

RECOMMENDATION

31 **Enable the local school community to take the problem-solving initiative.**

School districts can take several steps to support the site-level implementation of the recommendations in this report and to prepare and encourage the local school community to take the problem-solving initiative:

1. *Issue the invitation.* Jane David, Director of the Bay Area Research Group and one of the keenest observers of the school restructuring movement, notes that "perhaps the most critical" step in jump-starting the reform process in a school district is announcing—to all parties involved and in no uncertain terms—that the rules of the educational enterprise have changed and that what transpires at school will no longer be "business as usual." That invitation can take many forms. In the San Diego City School District with over 150 schools and 120,000 students, for example, the superintendent told his staff that, henceforth, no one at the district level—with the exception of himself or his deputy—could reject an innovative plan proposed by a school. The presumption was that site-based ideas were worth carrying out; the district staff's new charge was to figure out how to help the professionals at the school site do so. Other districts have created a climate that encourages innovation by awarding grants to schools proposing significant restructuring activities or by inviting them to create a provisional restructuring plan.

    One of the realities of institutional change is that it takes time to make it happen. Schools must be supported over a long enough period to allow the restructuring process to bear fruit. In order to encourage a spirit of creative risk-taking on behalf of the achievement of all students, administrators and school board members should adopt an attitude of understanding when well-conceived initiatives do not turn out satisfactorily. Tolerance for set-backs in the short term, however, should be matched by a constant rededication to long-term success—and decisive intervention in cases of persistent school-wide underperformance.

2. *Provide access to knowledge.* Providing guidance and assistance to teachers struggling to translate frameworks and model curriculum guides into a humming, daily classroom reality is a central challenge facing the elementary school reform movement. The district can assist teachers to meet this challenge in a number of ways.

    A key strategy in helping teachers in their quest for classroom improvements is to give them access to new knowledge about curriculum and instruction and the time to work out with their teaching colleagues how best to integrate that new knowledge in their daily activities. Accordingly, the Task Force has suggested that elementary schools take full advantage of the eight professional development days available to most of them. School boards and district administrators can play a key role in making this recommendation a reality.

Schools must be supported over a long enough period to allow the restructuring process to bear fruit.

Many schools that have seen the need for the eight professional development days have found their plans thwarted by a reluctant school board. Often this reluctance is based on the belief that support of the school's request will be unpopular with working parents who must arrange alternative day care or with parents who view professional development days as a waste of valuable instructional time. District administrators and board members can help remedy this situation in two ways. First, by publicly making the case for the importance of more staff development time, they can help create a climate in which parents understand and support the temporary inconvenience of increased student free days as an investment in long-term school improvement. Second, districts can help parents plan alternative activities for children on professional development days by (1) announcing the yearly calendar of the days well in advance; and (2) collaborating with other institutions in the community—the public library, local YMCA and YWCA, Boy Scout and Girl Scout troops, Boys Clubs and Girls Clubs, and so on—so that parents have a range of options. By eliminating the impediments to the use of staff development days, school districts can help ensure that individual schools take full advantage of this important resource.

3. *Make connections and run interference.* While the work of restructuring bears its fruit one student at a time, district offices can do much at the institutional level to prepare the way for the change efforts described in this report. For example, the economies and efficiencies of scale available at the district level can reduce the cost of bringing exciting new software to local schools. Likewise, the ability of the district's personnel office to recruit widely can increase the number of minority and bilingual teachers in the pool of candidates available to local schools.

Several of the recommendations in this report will be controversial in their implementation. School boards and district administrators must come to the support of local schools that have taken a stand for educational excellence for all students. For example, some schools attempting to include more literature in their English–language arts programs have found their reading selections under attack by those who would limit a child's access to some of the most engaging literature available. Likewise, many schools have faced strong challenges to their plans to reduce their reliance on ability-grouping as an instructional strategy by parents who fear a watered-down curriculum.

School boards and district administrators must come to the support of local schools that have taken a stand for educational excellence for all students.

Districts can lend strong institutional support to schools addressing controversial issues by making the district boardroom, rather than the school site, the arena for discussion and by ensuring that all interested parties have access to an established decision-making process.

4. *Grant real, not token, authority.* Finally, a school district shows its sincere commitment to the educational change process by what it no longer does in terms of making rules, issuing regulations, or prescribing policies that attempt to micro-manage how schools (or classrooms) are run. In principle, restructuring involves the granting of significant authority to the school site, usually through some type of representative body with decision-making power over such important areas as staffing, scheduling, instructional strategies, instructional materials, and budget matters. Unfortunately, Jane David has found, "examples of token authority—a small discretionary budget with specific requirements for planning and reporting— are far more common than examples of meaningful decentralization."[3] For many district offices, the restructuring process will require a basic shift in organizational culture: from one of promulgating rules and enforcing regulations to one of providing support and assistance for initiatives undertaken at the school site.

RECOMMENDATION

32 **Hold schools accountable for reaching agreed-on outcomes.**

Restructuring does not mean "everybody do your own thing." In a school district committed to the on-going restructuring process, schools are still expected to teach a rigorous thinking curriculum, such as that described by the state frameworks or in documents issued by leading national groups in the various disciplines. The purpose of restructuring is, after all, to improve student achievement. And even though districts may grant a substantial amount of autonomy to schools in teaching that curriculum, they must keep an eye on the academic bottom line and hold schools accountable for the achievement of all students at the school site.

Holding schools accountable means district administrators and school board members must accept responsibility for a number of specific activities:

1. *Build local support for statewide performance standards.* Chapter 4 of this report calls for the establishment of performance standards for elementary students at the state level that describe what students should know and be able to do. Such a set of standards in each discipline—clear, fair, and related directly to desired outcomes—

will enable schools and districts to speak a common language in setting goals and reaching them. District administrators and school board members should study the issues related to performance standards so they will be prepared to assume responsibility for establishing use of the standards at the local level.

2. *Establish local criteria for success.* Performance standards describe what California's students are expected to be able to do at various points in their educational careers. For example, in mathematics fifth grade students might be expected to make an accurate prediction about future events, based on a representative sample of past occurrences, and to demonstrate their reasoning graphically. Attainment of a performance standard is usually assessed by having students undertake a task that, when completed, demonstrates mastery of the performance standards. (See *Red Light, Green Light*, Chapter 4, page 69, for an example). How students do in such an assessment is usually reported on a scale (a scale of 6 to 1 is common), with each point on the scale accompanied by a descriptor identifying the traits of work at that level. In a given school, for example, the work of 11 percent of the fifth grade students might be judged as being "fully developed" (level 6) in meeting a particular mathematics performance standard, while the work of 60 percent of the students might be judged as adequate or better (level 4 or above). In holding individual schools accountable for student achievement, school boards and district administrators clearly have the responsibility for setting the criteria for success for each school. Is 60 percent of the students scoring at the adequate or above level acceptable for this school? If not, what is a reasonable goal for next year? For five years down the road?

3. *Make results public.* Holding schools accountable for the achievement of their students means that both goals and outcomes must be stated clearly and communicated widely. The use of performance standards, as called for here, is an obvious aid in this regard. Stating that "80 percent of the students at 55th Street Elementary School are able to write an acceptable persuasive essay" communicates much more to parents than saying "30 percent of our students score in the top quartile on a standardized test of reading." But being able to state things clearly and actually doing so are two different things. Districts must take the lead in making sure all who have an interest in the education of children have access to meaningful and understandable information about the achievement levels of individual schools.

In holding individual schools accountable for student achievement, school boards and district administrators clearly have the responsibility for setting the criteria for success for each school.

4. *Intervene in poor performing schools.* When results of performance assessments indicate that a school is failing, the school district is the child's first line of defense. Schools are offered professional development help or other services to build their capacity to do the job well. If the school continues in a tailspin despite this help, however, the district should intervene more directly—by changing the school's leadership, teaching staff, instructional strategies, or whatever else it takes to remedy the situation. The one alternative that is not acceptable is to do nothing in the face of persistent and chronic failure. Elementary school education is too important to the future prospects of young children to subject them to a foregone conclusion of educational insufficiency. All children can learn; and the district is the intercessor of first resort in seeing to it that California's elementary schools make sure that all children do.

For Further Information

David, Jane L. "What It Takes to Restructure Education," *Educational Leadership*, Vol. 48 (May, 1991), 11–15.

Elmore, Richard F., and others. *Restructuring Schools: The Next Generation of Educational Reform.* San Francisco, Oxford: Jossey–Boss, Publishers, 1990.

Lewis, Ann. *Restructuring America's Schools.* Arlington, Va.: American Association of School Administrators, 1989.

Making Schools More Effective: A Literature Review from Effective Schools to Restructuring. Prepared by Jane L. David and Patrick M. Shields, SRI International Planning and Evaluation Service, Office of Planning, Budget and Evaluation. Washington, D.C.: U.S. Department of Education, 1992.

"Restructuring Schools to Match a Changing Society," *Educational Leadership*, Vol. 45 (February, 1988), entire issue.

"Restructuring: What Is It?" *Educational Leadership*, Vol. 47 (April, 1990), entire issue.

ENDNOTES

Introduction

[1] The Los Angeles Unified School District collects data on over 80 different languages spoken by the students enrolled in its schools.

[2] Percentage of kindergarten enrollment provided through data collected in April, 1991, by Educational Demographics Unit, Program Evaluation and Research Division, California Department of Education.

[3] Kirst, Michael W., and others. *Conditions of Children in California.* Berkeley: Policy Analysis for California Education (PACE), 1989, p. 34.

[4] *Ibid.,* p. 50.

[5] "Explosive Growth, Dramatic Change for California Kids—and a Worsening Future Without Drastic Intervention," *Stanford Educator* (spring/summer, 1989), 1.

[6] Resnick, Laurel, and Leopold Klopfer. "An Overview" in *Toward the Thinking Curriculum: Current Cognitive Research.* 1989 Yearbook of the Association for Supervision and Curriculum Development. Edited by Lauren Resnick and Leopold Klopfer. Alexandria, Va.: Association for Supervision and Curriculum Development, 1989, p. 2.

Chapter 1: The Thinking Curriculum in the Elementary Years

[1] Examples are given by John Goodlad in *A Place Called School*, (New York: McGraw-Hill, 1983); and by William Bennett in *First Lessons: A Report on Elementary Education in America,* (Washington, D.C.: U.S. Department of Education, 1986).

[2] *Becoming a Nation of Readers.* Prepared by Richard C. Anderson and others. Washington, D.C.: The National Institute of Education, 1984, pp. 74–79; 119.

[3] *Ibid.,* p. 35.

[4] Porter, Andrew. "A Curriculum Out of Balance—The Case of Elementary School Mathematics," *Educational Research,* Vol. 18 (June-July, 1989), 9.

[5] *Getting Started in Science: A Blueprint for Elementary School Science.* National Center for Improving Science Education. Andover, Mass.: The Network, Inc., 1989, p. 39.

[6] Reprinted with permission from *Science for Children: Resources for Teaching* ©1988, National Academy of Sciences. Washington, D.C.: National Academy Press, 1988, frontispiece.

[7] Roth, Kathleen J. "Science Education: It's Not Enough to 'Do' or 'Relate,'" *American Educator,* Vol. 13 (winter, 1989), 16–22, 46–48.

[8] Based on data collected by the Center for Disease Control's Pediatric Nutritional Surveillance System as presented in *California Pediatric Surveillance: 1989 Summary Report.* Sacramento: Child Health and Disability Prevention Program, California Department of Health Services, 1989.

[9] Information gathered by the California Basic Educational Data System in October of 1990 showed that about 73,000 of the 3.6 million students in kindergarten through grade eight were taking a foreign language at some level of sophistication.

10 Among the challengers were Sidney Simon, Professor at the University of Massachusetts; and Jonathan Kozol.

11 Lickona, Thomas. *Educating for Character: How Our Schools Can Teach Respect and Responsibility*. New York: Bantam Books, Inc., 1991, p. 20.

12 Honig, Bill. *Last Chance for Our Children*. Reading, Mass.: Addison-Wesley, 1985, p. 95.

Chapter 2: In the Classroom

1 Caine, Renate N., and Geoffrey Caine. *Making Connections: Teaching and the Human Brain*. Alexandria, Va.: Association for Supervision and Curriculum Development, 1991, p. 5. Used with the permission of the authors.

2 *Curriculum and Evaluation Standards for School Mathematics*. Prepared by the staff of the Commission on Standards for School Mathematics, National Council of Teachers of Mathematics. Reston, Va.: National Council of Teachers of Mathematics, 1989.

3 Oakes, Jeannie. "Tracking: Can Schools Take a Different Route?" *NEA Today*, Vol. 6 (January, 1988), 45.

4 Resnick, Lauren. "Learning in School and Out," *Educational Researcher* (December, 1987), the 1987 presidential address.

5 Slavin, Robert. "Here to Stay or Gone Tomorrow: All About Cooperative Learning," *Educational Leadership*, Vol. 46 (December, 1989/January, 1990), guest editorial.

6 Pinnell, G. S. "Success for Low-Achievers Through Reading Recovery," *Educational Leadership*, Vol. 48 (September, 1990), 20.

7 Educational Demographics Unit, Program Evaluation and Research Division, California Department of Education.

8 *Program Advisory—Retention of Students in Elementary and Middle Grades*. Sacramento: California Department of Education, September 16, 1991.

9 *An Assessment of Educational Technology Applications in California Public Schools*. Chico: California State University, Chico, 1990.

Chapter 3: All in the Profession

1 Demographic data provided by the California Basic Educational Data System, as interpreted by the Educational Demographics Unit of the California Department of Education.

2 Lach, Michael. "Essay: An Inner City Education," *Scientific American* (January, 1992), 151.

3 Slavin, Robert. "Chapter 1: A Vision for the Next Quarter Century," *Phi Delta Kappan* (April, 1991), 588–589.

4 Demographic data provided by the California Basic Educational Data System, California Department of Education.

5 *Who Will Teach Our Children? A Strategy for Improving California's Schools: The Report of the California Commission on the Teaching Profession*. Dorman L. Commons, chair of the Commission. Sacramento: California Commission on the Teaching Profession, 1985, p. 13.

Chapter 4: Measures for Success

1 *California Assessment Program: Science Pilot Program*. Sacramento: California Department of Education, 1990. (Unpublished).

Chapter 5: Creation of a Learning Environment

[1] Caine and Caine, *Making Connections*, p. 81. Used with the permission of the authors.

[2] Olsen, Laurie. *Crossing the Schoolhouse Border: Immigrant Students and the California Public Schools.* San Francisco: California Tomorrow Project, 1988, p. 27.

Chapter 6: Coordinating Student Services

[1] *California: The State of Our Children 1991: What's Happening to Our Children?* Oakland: Children Now, 1991, p. 41.

[2] *Ibid.*, p. 24.

[3] Kirst, *Conditions of Children in California*, p. 323.

[4] *Ibid.*, p. 309.

[5] A memo issued December 28, 1990, by the U.S. Department of Education called for Head Start/school coordination.

Chapter 7: Organizing to Meet the Challenge

[1] Fullan, Michael. *The Meaning of Educational Change.* New York: Columbia University Teachers' College Press, 1982.

[2] Peters, Thomas J., and Waterman, Robert H. *In Search of Excellence: Lessons from America's Best-Run Companies.* New York: Harper and Row, Publishers, 1982.

[3] David, Jane L. "What It Takes to Restructure Education," *Educational Leadership*, Vol. 48 (May, 1991), 13.